NATIONAL RIFLE ASSOCIATION

RIFLE

INCORPORATED
1871

OF AMERICA

THE NRA

STEP-BY-STEP GUIDE TO
GUN SAFETY

HOW TO SAFELY CARE FOR, USE, AND STORE YOUR FIREARMS

THE
NRA
STEP-BY-STEP GUIDE TO
GUN SAFETY

HOW TO SAFELY CARE FOR, USE, AND STORE YOUR FIREARMS

Rick Sapp

Skyhorse Publishing books may be purchased in bulk at special discounts for sales promotion, corporate gifts, fund-raising, or educational purposes. Special editions can also be created to specifications. For details, contact the Special Sales Department, Skyhorse Publishing, 307 West 36th Street, 11th Floor, New York, NY 10018 or info@skyhorsepublishing.com.

Skyhorse® and Skyhorse Publishing® are registered trademarks of Skyhorse Publishing, Inc.®, a Delaware corporation.

Visit our website at www.skyhorsepublishing.com.

10 9 8 7 6 5 4 3

Library of Congress Cataloging-in-Publication Data is available on file.

Print ISBN: 978-1-5107-1405-2
Ebook ISBN: 978-1-5107-1406-9

Printed in China

You can join the NRA by contacting them at:

The National Rifle Association of America

11250 Waples Mill Road Fairfax, VA 22030

or by visiting their website, www.nra.org/museumoffer

CONTENTS

Welcome to a Lifetime of Fun

I believe in shooting and hunting, in owning and using firearms. I enjoy and promote this citizen's right and hope you will also and that you will do so safely.

Safe shooting provides a lifetime of fun, and so much more. We only need to pay attention to a few simple practices, principles that once learned become automatic.

The five million members of the National Rifle Association (NRA) are at the forefront of shooting and promoting shooting safety. And they have a proud record of achievement as well as activism. Perhaps you were not aware that:

• More than 120,000 certified NRA instructors train about 750,000 gun owners every year.
• Courses are available to teach the fundamentals of basic rifle, pistol, shotgun, and muzzleloading firearms, personal protection, ammunition reloading, and much more.
• Nearly 7,200 certified coaches are specially trained to work with young competitive shooters.
• Since the establishment of the lifesaving "Eddie Eagle GunSafe Program" in 1988, more than twenty-eight million pre-kindergarten to fourth-grade children have learned what to do if they see a firearm in an unsupervised situation.
• During the past seven years, "Refuse to Be a Victim" seminars have helped more than fifteen thousand men and women develop their own personal safety plan using common-sense strategies.

That's the broad picture of the NRA's commitment to firearms safety. As far as you and I are concerned, on a personal level, the NRA safety program can be summarized by a few relatively simple principles. Follow these and I can just about guarantee you a lifetime of fun.

1. <u>ALWAYS</u> keep the gun pointed in a safe direction.
This is the primary rule of gun safety. A safe direction means that the gun is pointed so that even if it were to go off it would not hurt anyone or damage something nearby. The key to this rule is to control where the muzzle or front end of the barrel is pointed all the time. And common sense dictates the safest direction, depending on the circumstances.

2. <u>ALWAYS</u> keep your finger off the trigger until ready to shoot.
When you're holding a gun, rest your finger on the trigger guard or along the side of the gun. Until you're actually ready to fire, don't touch the trigger.

3. <u>ALWAYS</u> keep the gun unloaded until ready to use.
Whenever you pick up a gun, immediately engage the safety and, if the gun has a magazine, remove it before opening the action and looking into the chamber(s), which should be clear of ammunition. If you do not know how to

Ensure your firearm is unloaded and pointing in a safe direction.

open the action or inspect the chamber(s), leave the gun alone and get help from somebody who does.

We live in an unusual time and place. With the world in turmoil, America has generally managed to honor its egalitarian principles and, though some people might disagree, to maintain the basic rights guaranteed to citizens in its founding documents. Freedom to worship as one pleases. Freedom to speak one's mind. Freedom against unreasonable searches and seizures. Freedom to own a firearm. These are precious liberties, ones that are rare in the world. Freedom together with other promises--such as freedom of assembly and of the press– is standard nowhere else.

It is not the responsibility of our government—local to national—to ensure our liberty, to maintain our rights as citizens. This responsibility belongs to us, to the

Always keep your finger off the trigger until you're ready to shoot.

citizens of the United States. It cannot be delegated or assigned, and it must not be ignored. It is our living entitlement to keep our freedoms alive, for us, for our children, and for their children. And every generation has to pay its dues.

These freedoms are a "package deal." By allowing one of them to be hedged about by government and its agents, we endanger them all. A minor infringement here to "ensure our safety," a small encroachment there to "promote the common good." Whatever the reason given, these minor adjustments to our liberties soon become wholesale opportunities to dismember our rights as citizens. And so I wholeheartedly support the Second Amendment, and the First and the Thirteenth, as well all of the other twenty-four.

Nevertheless, because it is entirely up to us to protect and promote our freedoms, we have to exercise what I like to think of as a "freedom opportunity." We can do this in a lot of ways: by considering the issues and the candidates for elective office, and then voting intelligently, and by speaking our minds with firmness, facts, and even passion. We can also protect our freedom by remembering that at every level, we the citizens created government, we are its masters; government did not create us and must not be allowed to define us.

In the case of the Second Amendment, our right to possess firearms, if we do not engage, do not own firearms, do not shoot and hunt, those who wish to remove this freedom from the Bill of Rights may do so at their leisure–and they will. Then, at some point, they may wish to eliminate freedom of assembly or our right to speak our mind.

In my experience, once these rights become abridged, the people don't get them back without a very long and unpleasant fight, if ever.

One of the principal ways we preserve and protect our opportunities to shoot and enjoy the outdoors with firearms is by safe shooting—practicing conscious safety at all times around guns. Mindfulness begins at the sales counter where dozens of firearms are on display. From the moment you first pick up your gun, it is crucial that you understand the responsibility and that you practice awareness. Begin your firearms handling or ownership with the end in mind—a lifetime of fun—and you will go a long way toward achieving that end.

We read, unfortunately, about someone who has handled a gun carelessly, forgotten the cartridge in the chamber of a semi-automatic or shot at movement in the bush rather than at an identifiable target. An accident can happen anywhere. And most accidents take place in settings and activities where accidents are easily preventable: at home.

A moment ago I mentioned that safe gun handling practices need to become automatic, and that's true. I believe that. But a new word has become popular lately that may better describe what I mean by "automatic," a word that is practically synonymous with awareness, and that is "mindfulness." It's a good word for us to apply to handling firearms. Mindfulness is a state of active, open

The Bill of Rights

The necessary two-thirds majority in both houses of Congress ratified the Bill of Rights on September 28, 1789. As sent to the states for approval, the Bill of Rights contained twelve proposed amendments to the Constitution. Amendments one and two did not receive the necessary approval from three-quarters of the states. As a result, amendment three in the original Bill of Rights became the first amendment to the Constitution. It and the remaining nine were ratified and made effective on December 15, 1791. This copy on vellum was signed by the Speaker of the House, Frederick Muhlenberg; the Vice President, John Adams; the Secretary of the Senate, Samuel Otis; and the Clerk of the House, John Beckley.

The Second Amendment is written as "Article the fourth: A well regulated Militia, being necessary to the security of a free State, the right of the people to keep and bear Arms, shall not be infringed."

concentration on the present, a state of living in the moment by giving it our complete attention.

Guns of all ages and sizes, shapes and calibers, have to be handled consciously, with awareness that they could be loaded. And thus someone could get hurt; someone could die if we're not being responsible. Even if you are absolutely certain that a gun is not loaded, handle it as if it were because you're forming a habit, and the consequences of a moment of inattention or carelessness can be disastrous.

I've often discussed our Second Amendment freedoms with celebrities who are rabidly anti-gun or with the media who claim to be—and sometimes truly are—unbiased when reporting a news story. Inevitably they all bring up some sad case of a recent accidental shooting, as if the story speaks volumes, speaks to the actions and even the intent of all of us who collect firearms and hunt with them and enjoy recreational shooting. Of course, they are wrong. The mainstream media neglect to report the countless stories of armed American citizens who successfully defend their families and property from those wishing to do them harm.

If you have an accident with a firearm however, whether or not anyone is injured, you can expect to be featured on the front page of the newspaper. You might very well find your story and any related photograph—something as meaningless as a picture of your home—syndicated by a national media network of which then says very ugly things about you. The facts may be incorrectly reported, half-true, and even distorted. Quite a number of unflattering characteristics may be attributed to you. This won't be personal, but it will feel that way.

The damage caused by carelessness is harmful to the entire firearms community in North America. It harms the twenty-five million hunters, competitors, and recreational shooters. It harms the fifteen million concealed-carry permit holders. It harms the 325 million citizens of the United States who believe in and honor our rights as citizens.

Carelessness with a firearm reverberates coast to coast because any unfortunate incident is endlessly repeated by the media—the more informed and the not-so-informed bloggers and hired pundits. The facts are often twisted to suit political and social objectives that may conflict with our liberties. Unsafe gun handling—and this could be careless storage or cleaning, as well as actively pulling the trigger—chips away not only at the Second Amendment, our right to bear arms, but at all of our liberties. Abridge our right to bear arms and it becomes easier to restrict our right to worship as we please or to speak uncomfortable truths to power.

And so I believe that safe gun handling, that lifetime of fun that I spoke of at the outset, is essential to preserving our lives, our liberties, and our pursuit of happiness. So be safe, be mindful, and keep shooting! Whether a hunter, a collector, or a target shooter, the best way for any firearms owner to understand gun safety is to know a bit of their history, how they are designed, and how they operate. That means we're going to take a look at each type of firearm. Just make sure to remember the fundamental rules of gun safety and how they apply to you. For a lifetime of fun, make them habits you and your family will practice for generations:

1. <u>ALWAYS</u> keep the gun pointed in a safe direction.
2. <u>ALWAYS</u> keep your finger off the trigger until ready to shoot.
3. <u>ALWAYS</u> keep the gun unloaded until ready to use.

Every American citizen is born with the right to keep and bear arms. Part of that right is a duty to store and use them carefully; respect your rights.

The Revolver

The revolver is a repeating firearm with a rotating cylinder containing multiple chambers and a barrel. We generally think of revolvers as handguns, but the revolving chamber design has also been applied to rifles and shotguns.

Inventors toiled for centuries in a quest to create a multiple-shot firearm. Firing, reloading, and firing a single-shot muzzleloader was a slow and tedious process. There had to be an easier way. Samuel Colt patented his first revolver in 1836. Though an unsuccessful venture at first, an order for one thousand guns from Captain Sam Walker of the Texas Rangers provided the capital and credibility needed to establish Colt as one of the premier firearm manufacturers in the world. Using the factories of Eli Whitney Jr., Colt fulfilled the order in 1847 and pioneered a method of mass production that would revolutionize American industry forever.

Early revolvers loaded powder and ball separately from the front of the cylinder (not from the front of the barrel like a musket). When loading, each chamber is rotated out of line with the barrel and charged from the front with loose powder and a slightly oversized ball that seals the chamber. The chamber is then aligned with the ramming lever underneath the barrel. Pulling the lever drives a rod into the chamber and seals the ball inside while holding the powder in place. Finally,

Historical Revolver

the shooter inserts his percussion caps and fires. After each shot, the shooter tilts his revolver vertically while cocking the hammer. Such a move allows for any fragments from the spent percussion cap to fall clear rather than clog the action. Faster than a single-shot muzzleloader, this was still quite a slow process. If you needed to fire quickly, these percussion-cap revolvers could not be effectively reloaded so people carried multiple guns or spare, pre-loaded cylinders.

In the late 1850s Horace Smith and Daniel Wesson (Smith & Wesson) developed revolvers that fired the first metallic cartridges. That is when the modern revolver truly came into being. Built with a fixed cylinder, these single-action revolvers incorporated a loading gate at the rear of the cylinder. The gate allowed loading one cartridge at a time. After a shot, the rod under the barrel pressed rearward to eject the fired case.

The operation of a revolver depends on having several firing chambers in a cylindrical block. Each time the revolver's hammer is cocked, the cylinder rotates to align the next chamber with the hammer and barrel. Chambers and cartridges are brought into alignment with the firing mechanism and barrel one at a time. In contrast, other repeating firearms—lever- and pump-action, and semi-automatics—use a single firing chamber and a mechanism that loads and then extracts cartridges.

Regardless of a revolver's shot capacity, each chamber is reloaded manually, which still makes reloading a revolver slower than reloading a semi-automatic pistol. A small-caliber revolver, such as the Smith & Wesson 617 chambered in .22 LR, holds ten rounds. A large-caliber revolver with large cartridges, such as the Smith & Wesson 460V in .460 S&W Magnum, holds fewer rounds.

Except for replica guns, like those used in cowboy-action shooting for example, which load a single cartridge at a time past the loading gate, modern handguns are generally built with swing-out cylinders. The cylinder mounts on a pivot that is coaxial with the chambers, and the cylinder swings out and down, usually to the left. An extractor is fitted, operated by a rod projecting from the front of the cylinder assembly. When pressed to the rear, the rod pushes shells out of the chambers simultaneously. The cylinder may then be loaded, singly by hand or with a speed-loader, closed, and latched in place.

Types of Revolvers

There are two basic types of revolvers, single-action and double-action. A single-action (SA) revolver requires you to pull the hammer back to manually cock it before each shot. Doing so revolves the cylinder to the next round and leaves the trigger with a "single action" to perform—releasing the hammer to fire the shot. That makes the effort and distance needed to actually pull the trigger minimal, but to fire a second shot, the hammer must be manually cocked again. The need to manually cock the hammer acts as a safety, as there is none built into the gun. The most obvious example of a single-action revolver is the Colt .45 Single Action Army, popularly known as "The Gun That Won the West."

Single-Action Revolver

With a double-action (DA) revolver, pulling the trigger moves the hammer back to the cocked position, indexes the cylinder to the next round, and then releases the hammer to strike the firing pin. You don't need to separately cock a double-action gun before pulling the trigger; every trigger pull completes the cycle. A double-action revolver can be fired faster than a single-action, but the additional effort required for the longer, harder trigger-stroke may reduce accuracy.

Most double-action revolvers may be fired in two ways and hence may be designated DA/SA, such as Smith & Wesson's 929. One firing mode is to cock the hammer with the thumb and then pull the trigger, single-action firing. The second is to simply pull the trigger from a hammer-down position, double-action firing.

Revolvers such as the Taurus CIA Model 650B2 are double-action only (DAO), sometimes referred to as "self-cocking." These handguns lack the

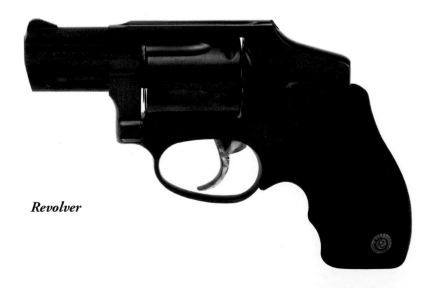

Revolver

Double-Action Semi Auto

latch that enables the hammer to be locked to the rear, and thus can only be fired in the double-action mode. With no way to lock the hammer back, DAO designs tend to have bobbed or spurless hammers; the hammer may even be completely covered by the revolver's frame. These guns are generally intended for concealed carry, because a hammer spur can snag on clothing when the revolver is drawn, especially if it is drawn hastily. The potential reduction in accuracy in aimed fire is offset by speed and increased concealment.

DA and DAO revolvers were the standard-issue police sidearm for decades, but in the 1980s the semi-automatic pistol took over this market. Semi-autos load faster and hold more cartridges or rounds; plus they often come with accessory rails for lights and lasers. Still, revolvers remain commercially popular because they are simpler to operate effectively, have greater overall reliability in difficult conditions, and can be kept loaded without fatiguing the springs.

The Semi-Automatic Pistol

"Pistol" designates a semi-automatic handgun, not a revolver, but the term is generally used to designate any handgun. The word pistol is thought to derive from Central European sources five or six hundred years ago.

Whatever the linguistic origin, semi-automatics have replaced revolvers for practically all military and law enforcement work, along with shooting games. In addition, the semi-auto is the handgun of choice for concealed carry. (The 9mm Beretta M9 has been the official pistol of the US military for twenty years.)

A semi-automatic handgun (sometimes called a self-loader) has only one chamber and barrel. Nothing revolves or rotates. Cartridges are loaded into a separate, reusable magazine that is inserted upward into the grip. Generally, cases are ejected and fresh cartridges load into the chamber by recoil energy or by using some of the hot, expanding gas from the previous shot. One bullet is fired and one empty case is ejected each time the trigger is pulled.

Most Americans accept that the semi-auto was invented by firearms designer John Browning, but the story is more complicated. The history of multi-shot firearms—usually meaning multiple barrels—may be almost a thousand years old. By the 1800s, quite a few Europeans were developing self-loading handguns in the era when Browning was learning the trade, Hiram Maxim, developer of the machine gun, Hugo Borchardt, Paul Mauser, and others.

It was Browning, however, who in 1896 moved the self-loading concept to the assembly line in cooperation with Belgian manufacturer Fabrique Nationale, and later in the US by Colt. Browning influenced nearly all categories of firearms design, but he contributed significantly to the evolution of auto-loading firearms. By inventing the telescoping bolt and integrating the bolt and barrel shroud into what is known as the pistol slide, his auto-loading pistols became both reliable and compact. Many of his century-old designs remain state-of-the-art.

Browning's M1911 single-action semi-automatic pistol, magazine-fed and recoil-operated, was a work of persistence and genius. Variants of the short-recoil M1911, originally in .45 caliber, but often modified in style and cartridge size, remain widely in use around the world. After World War II and two decades after Browning's death, most nations eventually adopted 9mm Parabellum caliber pistols employing Browning's locked-breech design as standard-issue military pistols.

Single-Action Semi Auto

Typically, the first round is manually loaded into the chamber by pulling back and releasing the slide mechanism, "racking the slide." After the trigger is pulled and the round is fired, the handgun's recoil or gas-feed operation extracts and ejects the shell casing and reloads the chamber.

Modern standard-issue semi-automatic pistols are usually double-action, also known as double-action/single-action (DA/SA). In this design, the hammer or striker may be cocked manually with the thumb or activated by pulling the trigger when firing the first shot. The hammer or striker is recocked automatically during each firing cycle.

In double-action pistols, the initial pull of the trigger requires significantly more pressure than subsequent firings. This is because the first pull also cocks the hammer, assuming it is not already cocked by hand.

Some modern semi-automatic pistols are double-action only (DAO). Each trigger pull fires a round until the gun and magazine are empty. This means that by pulling the trigger you cock the hammer (or striker or firing pin, depending on the gun's internal design) and release it to fire a cartridge in one continuous motion. Each pull of the trigger on a DAO semi-auto requires the same amount of pressure. DAO semi-automatic pistols are primarily recommended in the smaller, self-defense, concealable pistols, rather than in target or hunting pistols.

A single-action semi-auto must be cocked by first racking the slide or bolt, or, if a round is already chambered, by cocking the hammer manually. All SA semi-automatics exhibit this feature, and automatically cock the hammer when the slide is first racked to chamber a round. A round can also be manually inserted in the chamber with the slide locked back and then released to seat the round. Then the safety can be applied. The famed Colt M1911 is an example of this style of action.

Muzzleloading Rifle

The Rifle

A rifle is a long gun designed to be fired from the shoulder. Unlike a shotgun, a rifle fires a single projectile through a barrel that contains spiral grooves in its bore—the hole in the center of the barrel.

The rifle gets its name from a mechanical operation called rifling, cutting spiral grooves down the length of its steel bore. When the grooves are cut, they form a regular and continuous pattern of lands—the raised spots that the rifle bullet (or handgun bullet or the shotshell wad or sabot) contacts—and grooves. A rifling pattern of eight grooves, for example, will have eight lands. Lands and grooves can vary in number, depth, shape, direction of twist (right or left), and rate of twist.

Barrels are rifled to impart spin to the bullets. Because bullets are oblong objects, they must spin in flight, like a thrown football, or else they will tumble. This spin serves to gyroscopically stabilize the bullet, improving its aerodynamic steadiness and accuracy over the longer distances it is required to shoot.

Rifling is often described by "twist rate," indicating the distance the rifling needs to complete one revolution, such as "one turn in ten inches" (1:10 inches). A shorter distance indicates a "faster" twist, meaning that for a given velocity the projectile will rotate at a higher spin rate.

The combination of length, weight, and shape of a projectile determines the twist rate needed to stabilize it. Barrels intended for short, large-diameter projectiles such as spherical lead balls only require a low twist rate, such as one turn in forty-eight inches. Barrels intended for long, small-diameter bullets such as HSM's ultra-low-drag, 80-grain 0.223-inch (5.56 mm) bullets may need twist rates of one turn in eight inches.

The number of cartridge sizes, styles, compositions, and calibers for rifles (each rifle is chambered for a specific size and pressure) is immense. Big-game hunters (deer, moose, and bear) prefer to use rifles due to their greater accuracy and longer range. Rimfire rifles with smaller-caliber bullets are used to hunt small game (rabbits, coyotes, and squirrels), for informal target

shooting known as "plinking," and for competitive target shooting.

Rifles are the primary effective small arm of military forces. The legendary Russian AK-47 rifle is perhaps the most widely used and acclaimed military rifle ever produced, but many other rifles—the US M16 and variants among them—have their own fan base. No combat force would be complete without rifles.

Types of Rifles

Bolt-Action

The operator of a bolt-action rifle opens and closes the breech with a small handle that is attached to the bolt. Usually the bolt handle is built into the right-hand side because 90 percent of humans are right-handed. That means the hot, spent case is ejected to the right; it does not fly out and into the shooter's face. As the handle is operated, the bolt unlocks, the breech opens, the spent cartridge case ejects, the firing pin cocks, a new cartridge moves into the breech, and the bolt closes.

Bolt-action firearms are still popular for hunting and target shooting. Compared to most other manually operated firearm actions, bolt-action offers an excellent balance of strength (allowing powerful cartridge chamberings), reliability, and accuracy. They have a reputation for accuracy-at-distance and can also be cleaned faster than semi-autos because they have fewer moving parts. The major disadvantage is a lower rate of fire than lever- and pump-action guns, and a far lower rate of fire than semi-automatics.

Lever-Action Rifle

Bolt-Action Rifle

Lever-Action

The lever-action rifle uses a lever located around the trigger area to load fresh cartridges when the lever is worked. "Lever-action" generally implies a repeating firearm, but it is sometimes applied to some single-shot or falling-block actions that require a lever for cycling.

Lever-action rifles—which can be fired equally well by right- or left-handers—have fallen in popularity. Their heyday was the nineteenth century when Winchesters were seen in the scabbards of American cowboys.

The first significant lever-action design was Christopher Spencer's 1860 repeating rifle: magazine-fed, lever-operated, and breech-loaded. It was fed from a removable 7-round tube magazine, which, when emptied, could be exchanged for another tube.

Unlike later designs, early Spencer levers only unlocked the falling-block action and loaded a new cartridge from the magazine; they did not cock the hammer, which had to be cocked after the lever was operated. Also from 1860, the Henry rifle used a centrally located hammer that was cocked by the rearward movement of the bolt. The Henry placed the magazine under the barrel, rather than in the butt-stock, a development accepted by most tubular magazines since. By the 1890s, lever-action rifles evolved into a form that would last for a century. While they are not the most popular style of rifle today, they remain popular for hunters in heavily forested lands and have made a comeback in cowboy-action shooting.

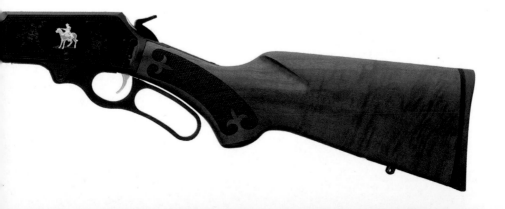

Pump-Action Rifle

Pump-Action

In a pump-action rifle (also called slide-action) the handgrip can be pumped back and forth to eject a spent round and chamber a fresh round. It is faster than a bolt-action or a lever-action, as it does not require the trigger hand to come away from the trigger while reloading.

Manual operation allows a pump rifle to rapidly cycle rounds of widely varying power that a gas- or recoil-operated firearm might fail to cycle. The simplicity of the pump relative to a semi-automatic also leads to improved durability and lower cost. Plus, the split second needed to work the action allows the operator to identify the target and aim. The pump is easy to use by both left- and right-handed users. The primary disadvantage of a pump is its relatively slow reloading time. Unlike pump-action shotguns, pump-action rifles are uncommon.

Semi-Automatic

A semi-automatic rifle fires a single bullet each time the trigger is pulled. It uses spent gases or recoil force to eject the spent cartridge, chamber a new round, and reset the action; this enables another round to be fired almost immediately after the trigger is pulled. The ability to automatically load the next round allows for an increase in the semi-automatic's rate of fire.

These rifles are also known as self-loading or auto-loading and are sometimes mistaken by poorly informed media or popular literature as automatic rifles or machine guns. An automatic, set to fire as long as the trigger is held down, can shoot until it is empty. A firearm with selective-fire capability, such as the M16, is built with a small lever that allows the shooter to select firing mode, usually one shot per pull of the trigger or a three-shot burst or even continuously.

Semi-Automatic Rifle

Semi-automatic rifles and automatic rifles appear similar.
Internal mechanics are the difference.

Semi-autos date from the German Mannlicher rifles of the late 1800s, but it took a generation before Winchester introduced them for civilian use. Perhaps the best-known semi-automatic rifle in the US is the famous locked-breech, gas-operated M1 Garand, the standard-issue infantry weapon used by American troops in World War II.

The semi-automatic uses a closed-bolt firing system in which a round must first be chambered manually before the weapon can fire. When the trigger is pulled only the hammer and firing pin move, striking and firing the cartridge. The bolt then recoils far enough rearward to extract and load a new cartridge from the magazine into the chamber, ready to fire again once the trigger is pulled.

Fully automatic firearms use an open-bolt mechanism. Pulling the trigger releases the bolt from a cocked, rearward position, pushes a cartridge from the magazine into the chamber, and fires the gun. The bolt then retracts to the rear to strip the next cartridge from the magazine (or the belt). The open-bolt system is often used in firearms with a high rate of fire such as sub-machine guns.

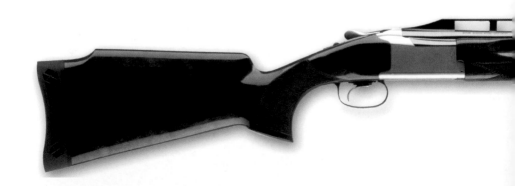

The Modern Sporting Rifle

The term "modern sporting rifle" or MSR describes semi-automatic rifles with detachable magazines—similar in design to the AR-15, which have been introduced to the US hunting and shooting market.

The MSR is semi-automatic only—one pull of the trigger equals one shot. With the customary attached rail systems, the MSR allows a variety of scopes, lights, and grips to be added.

The Shotgun

A shotgun is designed to be fired from the shoulder and uses the energy of a shotshell to fire a number of small spherical pellets called shot, or a solid projectile called a slug or sabot. Shotguns come in a wide variety of bore sizes, measured in "gauge." The smaller the number, the larger the bore and the larger and more powerfully loaded the shotshell—10-gauge being larger than 12- or 20-gauge.

Over/Under Shotgun

The 12-gauge is by far the most popular bore size with sportsmen. Smaller sizes or sub-gauges, especially the 20- and 28-gauge, have adherents among lightly framed individuals and shooting enthusiasts who enjoy the challenge of using a smaller load. In addition, the smaller bore sizes produce less blast and recoil. The 10- and 16-gauge are uncommon, though available, and the .410—properly referred to as a .410-bore rather than .410-gauge—is excellent for recreational shooting and introducing young people to shooting. (Shotshells for .410 are also used in recently designed handguns such as the Taurus Judge, as they are interchangeable in cylinders sized for .45 Colt cartridges.)

Like rifles or handguns, just describing styles and varieties of shotguns could fill entire volumes. Shotguns can be breech- or muzzle-loaded, single- or double-barrel, or a combination rifle/shotgun, pump-, bolt-, or lever-action, semi-automatic, and even fully automatic (military-only).

A shotgun is generally a smoothbore, which means the inside of the barrel is not rifled. The direct ancestor to the shotgun is the blunderbuss of Pilgrim fame. Shotguns were also used by cavalry troops due to their shorter length and ease of use on horseback.

Upon leaving the barrel, pellets spread out in a cone form. The power of the burning charge is divided among the pellets, which means that the energy of any single pellet is fairly low, but the impact of all or part is high. This makes shotguns especially useful for hunting birds and small game, where a few pellets will bring down a fast-moving target. In a military or law enforcement context, the large number of pellets in a shotshell makes the shotgun useful as a close-quarter-combat or defensive tool. Shotguns are also used for target-shooting disciplines—skeet, trap, and sporting clays—which require firing at flying (or bouncing) clay disks.

The history of the shotgun is almost as old as that of gunpowder. Smoothbore guns have been used extensively for centuries, but the earliest recoded use of the term "shotgun" was in Kentucky in 1776. Some designs, the double-barrel, for instance, have changed little in the last century. Modern innovations such as interchangeable chokes and sub-gauge inserts make the double-barreled shotgun the shotgun of choice in clay-bird shooting.

Semi-automatic shotgun

American inventor John Browning developed a lever-action repeating shotgun a few years later, followed soon after by a pump-action gun, and in 1900, the Browning Auto-5, the world's first semi-automatic shotgun.

Types of Shotguns

While there are a few niche muzzleloading shotguns like the Vintagers, most shotguns are of three types: the semi-automatic or auto-loader, the pump, and the break-action (double-barrel over/under or side-by-side, and single-barrel). The modern guns accomplish the basic operational steps of any firearm, but in slightly different manners.

The Semi-Automatic

While there are several manners of operation—long recoil, short recoil, and gas—a semi-automatic such as Remington's million-plus-selling Model 1100 is the most popular shotgun among American sportsmen.

Semi-automatics offer a variety of benefits. About one-third of perceived recoil is absorbed in operation of the action—tossing out the old shell and loading a new one—an especially attractive feature for young or novice shooters, those who fire hundreds of shots in a weekend competition, or waterfowl hunters firing magnum loads. Plus, a follow-up shot is almost instantly available and different barrels are easily interchangeable.

A semi-automatic has more moving parts than other shotgun types and thus requires more maintenance for continuous operation. Some semi-autos may experience trouble firing low-energy, reduced-load, and low-recoil rounds.

The Pump Shotgun

A pump-action shotgun such as the Mossberg 535 is cycled by "pumping" the forearm after a shot is fired. The forearm is connected to the breech-bolt by rods called action bars, which cause the bolt to move with the forearm. Pulling the forearm to the rear unlocks the bolt, extracts, and ejects the fired shell as

the forearm to the rear unlocks the bolt, extracts, and ejects the fired shell as the bolt moves rearward. Pushing forward then pulls the bolt forward and locks it in position. During its forward motion the bolt picks up a fresh shell from the magazine, pushes it into the chamber, and locks into place. The gun is then ready for another shot.

Pump-action shotguns are popular, reliable, and economically priced. They have a capacity for six or more shotshells and can be cycled quickly. Pump-guns are not popular for competition shooting because the act of cycling the forearm back and forth smoothly is not quickly mastered. Pump-action guns have a reputation for firing any properly sized load, heavy or light.

Break-Action Shotguns

Break-action shotguns come in single- and double-barrel versions. Single-barrel guns, sometimes with external hammers, are typically beginner guns or special-purpose competition guns. Double-barrel guns have the barrels placed side-by-side or one atop the other as an "over/under." For safety, the break-action gun can't be beat. Simply opening the action reveals whether it is loaded and renders it inoperable.

The side-by-side shotgun is popular worldwide, where, complete with fancy engraving decorated with gold and silver inlays, it becomes a family heirloom. A side-by-side such as Weatherby's 28-gauge Athena d'Italia is less common in the US, where over/unders such as Browning's famous Citori are more common. A side-by-side is nevertheless excellent for hunting birds and small game.

Double-barrel guns are almost always break-open designs. A top lever is pressed to the side and the barrels pivot down around a hinge pin. This opens the action and exposes the breech for loading and unloading. Most double guns have automatic ejectors, which propel fired shell cases out when the action is opened.

Generally, double-barrel guns have a set order in which barrels fire. This allows for the loading of two slightly different shells—a heavier, follow-up load if the first shell misses its target or the same shell with two differently choked barrels.

Pump-action shotgun

About Chokes

Shotguns use chokes to give the barrel's bore at the muzzle a very specific taper. Chokes help shape the spread and distribution of the shot for better range and accuracy. Chokes may be screw-in or fixed, depending upon the gun and its purpose.

For hunting most game birds and clay pigeons, for example, a desirable pattern is one that is as large as possible while also dense enough to ensure multiple hits on the target. A shotgun for home defense may be best with a smaller pattern and hence a tighter choke. The use of too much choke and a small pattern increases the difficulty of hitting the target; the use of too little choke produces large patterns with insufficient pellet density to reliably break targets or kill game.

Shotgun Chokes   *Shotgun Choke Tubes with Wrench*

About Ammunition

You need ammunition to shoot a gun. It sounds obvious, but a general understanding of ammunition is more complex than you might think. In general there are three types of ammo that are in use today: Self-contained metallic cartridges are used in handguns and rifles; self-contained shotshells are used in shotguns; muzzleloaders are used in a hand-loaded combination of powder, a paper wad or patch, and a ball or sabot shoved down the barrel with a ramrod. Let's see how everything comes together when you pull the trigger.

The Bullet

The projectile fired down the barrel of a modern handgun or rifle is a bullet. The primary element in a bullet is lead, but tin and antimony are also used to harden the relatively soft lead. Some bullets have a jacket of copper or gilding metal covering the outside for improved performance. Other materials are used in

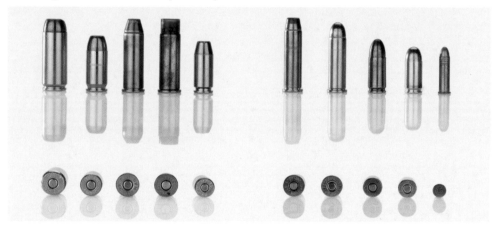

Pistol Cartridges and Case Heads

bullet manufacture today, including aluminum, bismuth, bronze, copper, plastics, rubber, steel, and tungsten—not to mention the copper and bronze bullets that have become increasingly popular.

Bullets are described by "caliber," or the diameter of a bullet, as well as design and weight. Caliber is expressed in hundredths or thousandths of an inch, or in millimeters.

Bullets come in a variety of shapes and constructions. Examples include FMJ (full metal jacket), JHP (jacketed hollow-point), and JSP (jacketed soft-point). Each bullet is built with specific options such as tip material and weight in grains (there are 437.5 grains per ounce). Bullets with a boattail design, for instance, have a beveled base that is reduced in diameter to improve air flow and stability in flight. Soft-nose and hollow-point bullets are designed to expand upon striking their target to intensify impact. Many rifle bullets have a sharply tapered front end or "nose." Most handgun bullets and some rifle bullets have a round nose. Competitive pistol shooters may use flat nose bullets to punch cleaner holes in paper targets.

Do some research before deciding which bullet best fits your needs.

Unlike a rocket, a bullet is not a self-powered projectile. The power for bullet flight comes from rapidly expanding hot gas created by burning powder confined in the barrel behind it. The study of bullet flight is called ballistics.

Between the ignition of the propellant and the bullet's exit from the muzzle, its jacket engages the twisting lands of land-and-groove rifling inside a barrel and it begins to rotate in a predictable manner. This rotation gives it stability and accuracy.

Because most bullets contain lead, it is important to be thorough about hand washing. If you are hand loading or casting your own bullets, an area that excludes children and provides good ventilation is a must.

The Propellant

The burning powder that propels a bullet downrange is "propellant." Propellants are carefully formulated for expansion rate, physical size and shape of the tiny powder particles, and inherent stability. These are important factors for producing specific propellants for specific firearms and purposes. As you might imagine, propellants were not invented overnight.

A type of gunpowder known as "black powder" is composed of a nitrate salt (saltpeter), sulfur, and charcoal, and is believed to have originated in China a thousand years ago. This form of gunpowder readily absorbs moisture and can explode unexpectedly. It also produces a great volume of smoke and fouling inside the barrel when ignited, and so has been replaced by modern "smokeless" powders.

The move to smokeless powder began about 125 years ago, coinciding with the development of primers and self-contained cartridges. Why do we call it smokeless powder? Because this version of gunpowder produces a significantly less amount of smoke than black powder.

Today, commercial smokeless powder comes in two varieties; single-based powders are made of nitrocellulose and double-based powders are made of nitrocellulose and nitroglycerine. These components contain small amounts of other chemicals, and each granule is coated in graphite to make it easier and safer to handle.

Propellants are also classified by kernel structure: their geometric design as flakes, spheres, or cylindrical sticks. Their burn rate is controlled by composition and by perforating them or coating the kernels with a retardant.

A particular burn rate will suit a particular type of firearm and typically will be designated for either rifles, handguns, or shotguns.

Bullet weight, shape (or styling), and caliber are printed on every retail cartridge box, but not the type or amount of propellant. Unless you reload cartridges (also called hand loading) or study ballistics, propellant data is irrelevant.

Still in use by shooters who enjoy the mystique of older muzzleloaders, black powder is volatile and must be kept cool, dry, and stored under lock-and-key. While modern powders will not explode, they will burn rapidly. If you have gun powders in the home, they should be locked in a separate area from your living quarters. And always wash your hands and the work area carefully after handling raw powders.

The Case

Although you will find some rifle and pistol cases that are manufactured of aluminum and steel, most small-arms ammunition cases are a brass alloy. These cases—commonly referred to as "brass"—are made in sizes and shapes for specific types of guns, but they have a generic function: Hold the primer,

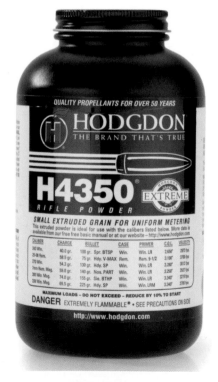

Hodgdon Propellant   *Cutaway Pistol, Rifle, and Shotgun Cartridges*

the propellant, and the bullet. The cartridge case seals the firing chamber in all directions except the bore. A case makes handling ammunition easy, and once all the components are in place in the case, it becomes a cartridge.

Naming cartridges is a 150 year-old game in which no internationally accepted standard exists. A .45-caliber pistol may be a .45 ACP or .45 GAP, .45 Long Colt or even .454 Casull. The popular 9mm (.354 inches) handgun caliber is actually called 9x19 Parabellum (or 9mm Luger) to differentiate it from other guns using a 9mm bullet, like the .380 ACP (also called the 9mm Short, 9mm Kurz, and 9mm Corto), which has a much shorter case. It is important for effective shooting and for your personal safety to use the correct ammunition for your gun.

Case design is determined by the firearm in which the ammunition is used. Some handgun-caliber cases are nickel-plated for durability in reloading, corrosion resistance, and appearance. Each case is stamped with caliber and manufacturer, and your firearm will safely accept only certain types of cases as specified in the Owner's Manual.

Generally, every characteristic of a specific cartridge type is tightly controlled and few are interchangeable.

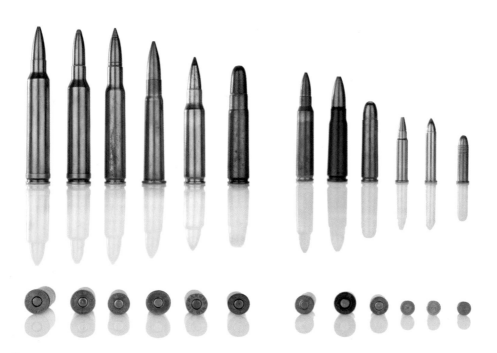

Rifle Cartridges and Case Heads

The Primer

Two types of cartridges, rimfire and centerfire, relate to the style of primer used. Pull the trigger and a gun's firing pin hits the impact-sensitive primer to create a tiny explosion that ignites the propellant and forces the bullet out of the case downrange.

A centerfire cartridge has a centrally located primer. Most US-manufactured centerfire brass cases use Boxer primers, which can easily be removed and replaced after firing using standard reloading tools. European cartridges use Berdan primers, a slightly different style.

The entire inside bottom edge of a rimfire cartridge is the primer. This design is less expensive to manufacture, but once fired the case is permanently deformed and can't be reloaded. A modern rimfire gun is designed for small calibers, a ".22 Long Rifle," for instance, but not for larger rifle or pistol cartridges.

Centerfire primer cups are made of soft copper or brass alloy, and are nickel-plated to resist corrosion, with a brass anvil inside. They are filled with impact-sensitive chemical compounds. When struck by the firing pin, the center of the cup collapses, squeezing the explosive between its inner surface and the anvil. This burst of heat shoots a flame through the flash hole, igniting the propellant to fire the cartridge.

The Shotshell

Unless a barrel is specifically rifled for a slug or sabot round, shotguns are smoothbores. A rifled barrel increases the accuracy of slugs, but makes the barrel unsuitable for firing shot. The self-contained shotshell cartridge is both different from and similar to a metal cartridge. The similarity is that both contain a primer and propellant in a case. The differences are the case design and construction, the use of loose shot instead of a single bullet, and extra internal components such as a wad, an overlay card, or even shot-buffering material.

The shotgun cartridge begins with a brass base containing a hollow plastic case. (Paper cases, once common, are now rare.) Into this centerfire case is loaded a shotgun primer, a propellant, a wad, and shot. The lip ("mouth") of the case is then folded (crimped or rolled) over to hold everything in place.

After the powder, the round wad—paper, plastic, or fiber—is inserted to prevent shot and powder from mixing, provide a cushion against shot deformation, and provide a seal that prevents gas from blowing through the shot rather than pushing it forward. Plastic wad designs often incorporate a shock absorber with a cup that acts as a spacer and holds the shot together until it is out the barrel. Shot cups also have slits on the sides so that the wad will peel open and fall away after leaving the barrel, allowing the shot to continue on in flight undisturbed.

Shotgun Shell Cutaways

Shotgun Shells and Case Heads

Whereas rifles and handguns are measured by caliber, shotguns and shotshells are measured by gauge (or bore). This is both a more antique system and more complicated than simply measuring the diameter of the barrel interior. In its antique description, gauge is the weight, in fractions of a pound, of a round lead ball that is the same diameter as the internal diameter of the barrel. Thus a shotgun is called 12-gauge because a lead sphere that just fits the inside diameter of the barrel weighs a twelfth of a pound. A 10-gauge has a larger-diameter barrel than a 12-gauge, and a 20-gauge is smaller. Commercial shotguns come in six gauges, largest to smallest—10-, 12-, 16-, 20-, 28-, and .410 (actually a caliber designation of .410 inches). Some shotshells are available in different case lengths. Using shotshells longer than the gun is designed to accommodate will create very dangerous pressure on firing. Never place shotshells of a smaller gauge in a larger gauge shotgun. A 20-gauge shotshell, for example, will lodge in a 12-gauge barrel far enough down the barrel to permit a 12-gauge shotshell to be loaded behind it. If fired, the result will be, at best, a ruptured barrel. It is vital to use only shotshells designed for your size shotgun.

A shotshell can be loaded with a variety of small round shot, lead being traditional, or steel, bismuth, or tungsten alloys, the latter groups now required for waterfowl hunting. Shot is available in different sizes and is selected depending on the target or task. For short-range skeet shooting, a small-diameter shot such as #9 shot (.079 inches in diameter) is preferable for a high-density pattern. Trap shooting requires longer shots, and so larger #8 or #7 1/2 shot is used to provide sufficient energy to reliably break the target. For hunting, the range and the penetration needed to ensure a clean kill must both be considered. For dove, use #8 (.089 inches), but for turkey, #4 (.129 inches) or larger is needed. For self-defense, buckshot is preferable, #2 Buck (.27 inches) up to double-ought Buck measuring .33 inches.

Muzzleloading

Until the nineteenth century, the only way to load a firearm—a rifle, pistol, or shotgun—was to first pour the black powder down the barrel, then place a greased cloth patch around a lead bullet, and shove the bullet down the barrel, seating it next to the powder, with the ramrod. A flintlock produces a small spark and a percussion cap produces a small explosive flash to ignite the powder which fires the bullet. Loading is a slow process and both the load and the process used must be consistent to obtain an accurate shot. After repeatedly firing, the barrel could become fouled to the point that loading becomes impossible. Cleaning the bore between shots prevents this problem.

By the end of the nineteenth century, breech-loading firearms replaced most muzzleloaders, except for black-powder enthusiasts and reenactors (a person who reenacts historical battles or events). Modern muzzleloading firearms include reproductions of flintlock, and percussion long guns and pistols and "in-line" rifles that use a closed breech, sealed primer, and fast rifling for accuracy at long ranges.

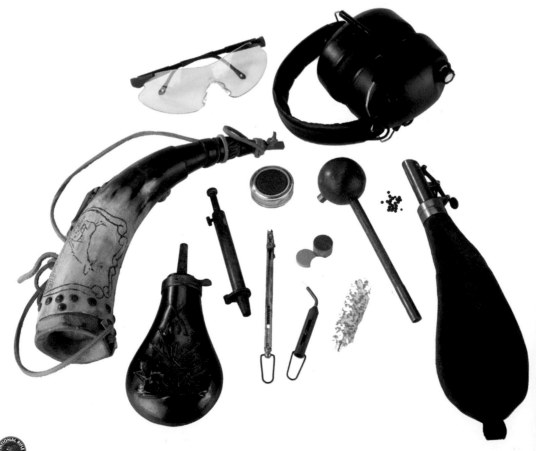

Muzzleloading essentials

Several design changes have brought muzzleloading firearms back for a percentage of hunters and recreational shooters. The saboted (plastic encased) bullet, for instance, which simplifies and expedites loading, has become a projectile of choice among non-traditional muzzleloader hunters, because it is a more accurate projectile. Secondly, Hodgdon's Pyrodex pellets are extraordinarily convenient. Instead of measuring loose propellant into a muzzleloader's muzzle, you simply drop in one or more pellets, depending on the caliber, bullet weight, and velocity required. Tedious measuring and spillage are eliminated.

NEVER use smokeless powders in a muzzleloading gun. They are not made to withstand the increased pressure that develops on firing.

Hornady® MonoFlex®
Bullets .50-cal. Sabot

Hodgdon Pyrodex Muzzleloading
Propellant and Goex Black Powder

Hodgdon's pelletized Pyrodex premeasured propellant

WHAT TO WEAR SHOOTING

Shooting, like voting, is one of the most democratic of activities. America's founding documents, the bedrock of our society, discuss firearms in the same breath as freedom of speech and religion. There is no mention of proper dress and etiquette, even though the founders inherited a very strict and inflexible class-oriented code from their European ancestors . . . including powdered wigs for men.

When you think of dressing for a day of shooting, some may think of an English horseman riding to hounds. Red coats flashing. Bugles blaring. Hounds barking. In America, except for a few clubs whose members enjoy maintaining this staid tradition, formal shooting get-ups seem pretentious.

Still, only a century ago, American gentlemen would often wear a coat and tie for a day of shooting. The Order of Edwardian Gunners, less formally known as the Vintagers, for example, is organized for the appreciation and collection of Edwardian-era (1880 to 1914) side-by-side shotguns and rifles. Times do change, but we all like dressing up now and then.

36   *Hunter wearing blaze orange*

Orange, the New Black

That said, there are a few general rules and a number of recommendations—some for safety, but mostly for comfort—for a day of shooting, and they begin with color.

We have all seen hunters wearing "blaze orange" with their camouflage gear. Against a patterned background such as a forest, bright orange is undeniably attention getting. This vivid orange hue is sometimes referred to as safety orange, or OSHA orange, so called because it is required attire by the Occupational Safety and Health Administration for many occupations. Its use is designed to set objects apart from their surroundings—traffic cones in construction zones, clay pigeons for trap shooting—a particularly effective contrast to the azure color of the sky on a summer day. (On the color wheel, azure and orange are complementary colors, creating a very strong contrast between the two.) There is even a national standard for hunter, or blaze, orange known as ANSI standard Z535.1-1998 for Color #12199. (More on ANSI standards in the "Firearms Storage" chapter.)

Every US state and Canadian province has some regulation about wearing blaze orange by gun hunters and sometimes by archers as well. Bands of blaze orange must also be wrapped around the barrel tips of replica guns such as airsoft guns, and cap pistols or toy guns.

Clothing—for Comfort

When shooting in a competition, there may often be rules for special venues, but overall, clothing is designed for comfort. Padded vests, for instance, will be worn by shotgun and rifle competitors to help reduce the bruising of their shoulders during a Camp Perry rifle match or even a day of dove shooting. The thin, decorative pad on the vest complements the more functional recoil pad (butt pad) on the gun. The theory perhaps is that if you are comfortable, you are less inclined to hold the gun in an unusual and unsafe position.

Any shooter who fails to wear proper eye and ear protection is asking for trouble that is easily and inexpensively averted. Eye protection is always recommended while shooting to help prevent flying particles from reaching the eye.

Should you wear gloves when handling firearms? This is a personal decision based on whether gloves give you a better "feel for" or purchase on the firearm. Generally, any clothing item that helps one handle a gun safely and with confidence is recommended. The gloves should be washed periodically according to manufacturer instructions. (You should always wash your hands and face after shooting. A good washing with soap and water will remove lead and combustion particles.)

Otherwise, clothing for shooting generally matches the season and the sport. One might wear a cap, vest, and glasses for a day of pheasant hunting, a popular camouflage base for a day in the deer woods, but a morning of

Always wear protective eye and ear wear.

shooting at an indoor range requires little more than safety glasses and hearing protection. A separate clothing issue is often raised by women who have for years complained that shooting clothing does not match their physique. Men are, on average, taller, heavier, and shaped differently than women. These days, a number of garment manufacturers like Próis Hunting & Field Apparel for Women have decided to address that issue by designing clothing to accommodate the special needs and features of women shooters.

Today's shooter can be seen wearing every style available on the street, from hardcore camouflage addicts, to flip-flops and cut-off jeans, to a dress and heels. The garments only need to match the shooting situation. As a general rule, comfort and some thoughtfulness for fellow shooters are the primary considerations.

A number of companies now make clothes that are designed to fit a female physique and to maximize comfort out in the field.

Low profile hearing protecion

The Noise We Hear

Firearms are incredibly loud. When the powder burns, almost instantaneously, we understand why 10 percent of the American public experiences some form of hearing loss. Unlike the sustained roar of a rock concert, measured at 110 to 120 dB (decibels), for a split second a gunshot can exceed 160 dB—140 dB is considered the "threshold of pain." This is far beyond what the US government says is safe for an unprotected on-the-job worker.

Normal conversation occurs at about 60 dB. Lawn mowers run at 90 dB, a jet engine at 140 dB, and the searing noise on a rocket pad during launch pushes the top end of the scale past 180 dB. A gunshot is typically in the 150 to 160 dB range. Although it is very intense, its duration is short.

According to OSHA, the federal Occupational Safety and Health Administration, even sound spikes of 130 dB, lower than most firearm reports, may instantly cause permanent damage in the inner ear. And so every shot has the potential of damaging your hearing, not your ears per se, but the delicate and irreplaceable hairs inside your ears that modulate and transmit sound. Cause them to wither by continuous unprotected shooting or any continuous unprotected exposure to extremely loud noise . . . and you're deaf. Forever. Because hearing loss is painless and gradual, it can go unnoticed until the loss becomes severe. Unlike biceps built up by lifting weights or quads that grow stronger when we run, ears do not get tougher with exposure to noise; after a while they simply stop working.

A symptom of sustained loud noise is tinnitus, a persistent ringing in the ears, even when no sound is actually present. This condition can become permanent and more than annoying; it can be socially debilitating and painful.

Protect Your Hearing

It's easy, it's not expensive, and it's no longer "macho" to refuse hearing protection.

These days, no public range will allow you to shoot without a minimum of ear (and eye) protection. This typically means they hand out, often free, sets of disposable soft plastic or foam earplugs. Even these minimal plugs can have a noise-reduction rating (NRR) of 30 dB; their use drops the noise of a 160 dB shot from about to 130 dB, almost 20 percent.

The beauty of soft, disposable earplugs is that they are extremely cheap, easy to fit in almost anyone's ear canals, and effective at bringing the noise of a shot below the threshold of pain, even into an acceptable range for a "normal" day of shooting. They are sold in every sporting goods and hardware store in the nation. Curiously, more elaborate (and more expensive) earplugs made in dramatic shapes, often with cords attached and backed by carefully researched science, do not produce a significantly higher level of sound muffling than the most basic foam, properly inserted disposables if in both ears.

It's easy to believe that ear-protecting, over-the-head muffs are a step up from simple earplugs. Ear muffs will last for years, but they provide no more noise reduction than basic foam plugs, 20 to 30 dB. One of the difficulties with muffs—however they are branded—is that they become hot on a warm day and a shooter begins to perspire under the rubberized cups.

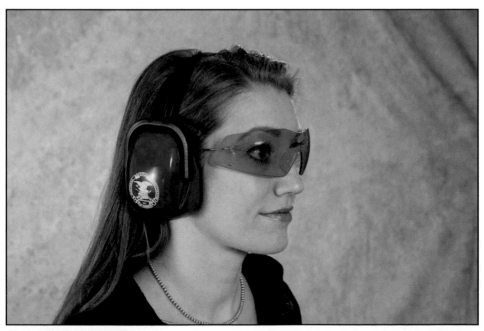

Over-the-head muffs

Soft disposable earplugs

Roll the earplugs for inserting into your ear.

Intuitively, using earplugs and muffs, one might think it should double your protection to about 60 dB, but this is not so. The actual or "heard" reduction is perhaps another 5 to 10 dB for a total NRR using both muffs and earplugs of 35 to 40 dB. Nevertheless, in protecting those tiny interior ear hairs, the actual instruments that allow us to hear, this is an excellent personal choice.

An increasingly popular option is the use of electronic hearing-protection devices, including specialized hearing aid/earplug combinations, and earmuffs fitted with external microphones and internal speakers. You might notice such muffs equipped with a microphone and used by a tour guide in a crowded museum or someone walking along a noisy road wearing earmuffs, the muffs sporting an antenna so the exerciser can listen to the radio or perhaps communicate with the office.

The sound-dampening system in electronic muffs allows the wearer to hear surrounding sounds or the radio even louder than normal, because volume is controlled by a dial on the muff shell. When dangerously loud sounds are detected by the electronics, the speakers to the ears deactivate until the noise falls once again to a predetermined safe level. The Elvex Level Dependent muff, for example, has an "impulse filter" that electronically eliminates impulse sounds such as a gunshot by closing the circuitry in four milliseconds, and then opening it again in about one-quarter second (to prevent any echo effect). Thus an electronic muff combined with a simple foam earplug might give the very best possible hearing protection on range, at a shooting competition, or while hunting.

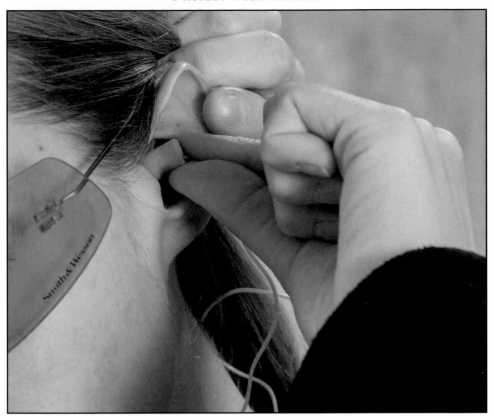

Gently insert into your ear.

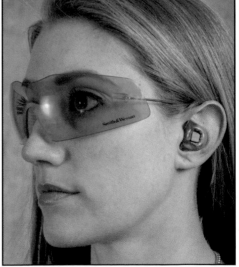

NRA ZEM enhanced hearing protection   Custom-molded ear plugs

PROTECT YOUR EYESIGHT

"But I already wear glasses!"

Yes, and in a sport where participants are highly encouraged to wear eye protection, your glasses are certainly better than nothing. It can happen in any number of ways; splash-back from steel targets, debris from the shooter's gun at the shooting station next to you, or smoothbore pellets from the hunter who nails a thunder chicken (pheasant) flying a little too close can cause some serious damage. It is also a good idea to consider eye protection before a splash of cleaning solvent at your workbench calls for an emergency visit to the hospital.

(This is an opportune moment to emphasize hand washing—soap and hot water—after reloading ammunition, shooting, or handling guns and ammunition. A personal scrubbing will remove lead, barium, and antimony, the customary by-products of shooting.)

Adjust hearing protection to accommodate shooting glasses.

Covering Your Eyes

It costs almost nothing to completely protect your eyes. Comfortable eye protection is cheap, less than ten dollars at mass merchants. Expense is not an excuse for not wearing eye protection.

As well as providing impact protection, some shooting glasses can protect your eyes from harmful solar rays by absorbing or reflecting at least 99 percent of UV radiation.

A common discussion among shooters is what color lens is best, but of course there is no single answer. Browning applies its brand to shooting glasses and says that a buyer should expect good-quality shooting glasses to come with interchangeable lenses. Generally, lens color is recommended as follows:

Clear glasses are recommended for indoor ranges.

Smoke: For bright days, smoked lenses reduce glare but transmit all colors at the same level. Smoke does not enhance orange targets.

Clear: Best for poorly lighted areas such as indoor ranges, and when eye protection is worn over prescription glasses. Clear lenses provide no contrast. They are an excellent safety lens color when handloading ammunition.

Yellow: Excellent for overcast or foggy days or late afternoon. Good for rifle or pistol shooting with black-and-white targets, they appear to brighten indoor ranges.

Orange: Enhances the orange of orange clay targets and shooting on dull, cloudy days, or at dusk or dawn when game animals are on the move.

Vermillion (red): Superior for green backgrounds, vermillion also highlights orange while dampening green and blue. Good for those who see orange poorly or shooters who have deficiencies in the red-green color spectrum.

Brown: This is a light-reducing lens. Good all around for shooting orange targets on bright, glaring days with open backgrounds.

Photo chromatic "transition" lenses: These lenses darken in response to bright ambient light.

Rx lenses: Many high-end eyewear sets offer the ability to attach prescription lenses, an option of special interest to older shooters. (Your local optician can facilitate this.)

Polarized lenses: Action shooters may find that polarized lenses cut glare and help define their target.

Shooting Glasses with interchangeable orange, yellow, clear, smoke, and blue lenses (see next page).

SAFE GUN HANDLING

In a book that is all about safety—about a lifetime of fun owning, collecting, handling, and, yes, even cleaning firearms—it is important to note that hunting, competition, and recreational shooting are among the safest of all sports. Surprised? This may sound counterintuitive, certainly paradoxical because unlike a set of downhill skis or a tennis racquet, a gun can cause damage if not used correctly. In clay-target sports like trap and skeet, a gun is used to crush flying clay disks called pigeons or birds. In hunting, a gun is used to "harvest" game animals.

Shooting with a firearm is a safe sport primarily because those who love it insist upon safety. Safe gun handling is required at every venue where firearms are involved, from the casual weekend gun show to national trap competitions. Shooting is safe because if you experience a moment of carelessness, the man or woman standing next to you is going to correct you—and they expect that you will do the same for them, should they point their gun in an unsafe direction or fail to break open their shotgun when returning to the clubhouse. Such corrections are not a personal commentary. They are not a slight on your character (unless the unsafe practice is repeated), but are an instance of "cooperative ownership," an instance where firearms enthusiasts self-regulate and police our own ranks. As a gun owner, you will also be expected to do your part, to be an ambassador for safe gun handling.

Shooter being instructed by NRA safety officer to keep the gun pointed in a safe direction.

Safe gun handling and usage is a responsibility of every hunter. Having a partner for an extra set of eyes adds an extra layer of safety.

The National Shooting Sports Foundation (NSSF) has compiled national data indicating that hunting ranks third in safe sports when compared to twenty-eight other recreational pursuits, ranging from baseball to wrestling. Hunting with firearms has an injury rate of .05 percent, which equates to about one injury per two thousand participants, a safety level bettered only by camping (.01 percent) and billiards (.02 percent). By comparison, golf has an injury rate of .16 percent (one injury per 622 participants). Tackle football, by the way, topped the list of dangerous activities with an injury rate of 5.27 percent (one injury per nineteen participants). To put hunting's safety standing into perspective, the NSSF notes that compared to hunting, a person is:

• Eleven times more likely to be injured playing volleyball.
• Nineteen times more likely to be injured snowboarding.
• Twenty-five times more likely to be injured cheerleading or bicycle riding.
• Thirty-four times more likely to be injured playing soccer or skateboarding.
• 105 times more likely to be injured playing tackle football.

Although the count appears to be on the low side, the number of licensed hunters who went afield last year is estimated at more than sixteen million, including three million archers who hunt with the bow and arrow. Of that total, approximately 8,122 sustained reported injuries, or fifty injuries per one hundred thousand participants, anything from tripping over their own feet and twisting an ankle to a fatal fall from a treestand.

The vast majority of hunting accidents—more than 6,600—were treestand-related, hunters hurt when climbing into or out of a commercial or homemade platform. Accurate figures on recent fatalities related to hunting are not available, but statistics from the 2002 season indicate there were ninety-nine fatal hunting accidents that year.

You might also be surprised to learn which popular sports are most injury-prone. Compiling 2010 information from the National Electronic Injury Surveillance System of the Consumer Products Safety Commission, the International Hunter Education Association's Hunter Incident Clearinghouse, and the National Sporting Goods Association Sports Participation Survey, the most accident-riddled sports are (in order of danger—percentage of injury per one hundred participants): tackle football (5.27), basketball (1.96), skateboarding (1.70), soccer (1.68), wrestling (1.47), bicycle riding (1.33), baseball (1.30), cheerleading (1.25), softball (1.11), and snowboarding (.94). And remember that hunting with a firearm ranked .05!

It is not only in America's fields and forests that firearms are being used safely, though. The most recent data (2008) from the Centers for Disease Control and Prevention report that firearms constitute just half of 1 percent of all unintentional fatalities in the US, including those in the home. Apparently, as long as participants maintain a mindful, conscious awareness of safe gun-handling practices, shooting in all of its forms is a safe activity.

Guidelines for Gun Safety

Safety is fundamental to all shooting activities. Whether you're practicing at the range, hunting in the field, or cleaning your gun in your workshop, the rules of firearm safety always apply.

Safe gun handling involves the development of knowledge, skills, and attitude—knowledge of the gun safety rules, the skill to apply these rules, and a safety-first attitude that arises from a sense of responsibility and an understanding of potential dangers.

Most gun accidents are caused by ignorance and/or carelessness. Ignorance is a lack of knowledge—a person who handles a gun without knowing the gun safety rules or how to operate the gun is exhibiting a dangerous lack of knowledge. Equally dangerous is the person who, although knowing the gun safety rules and how to properly operate a gun, becomes careless in properly

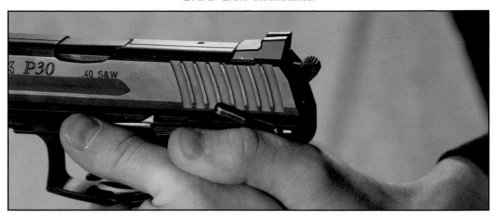

Right-handed grip showing the thumb-mounted safety selector in the ON position.

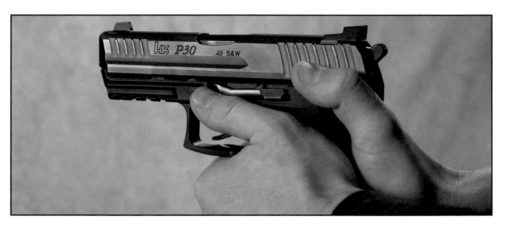

Thumb-mounted safety selector being turned to the OFF position.

This shooter has a firearm in a high compressed position with his finger off the trigger and the thumb-mounted safety selector in the OFF position.

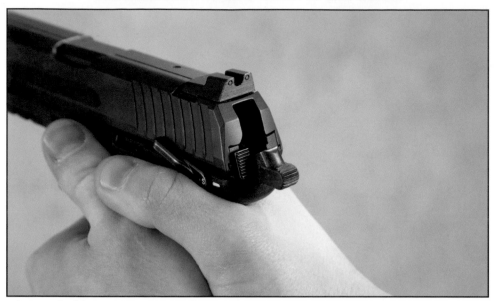

Shooter holding a firearm, with a cocked hammer and the safety engaged.

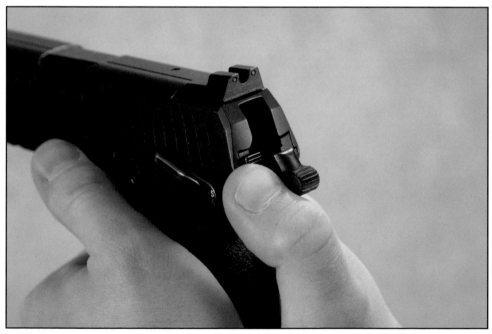

Shooter pressing the decocker button on the back of the slide to safely lower the hammer. When using a pistol with these types of controls (see previous photos) it is recommended that you put the safety in the ON position, if applicable, before decocking the pistol. Note: A mechanical safety uses a device that may break or fail; therefore, it is imperative that you follow the NRA Three Gun Safety Rules.

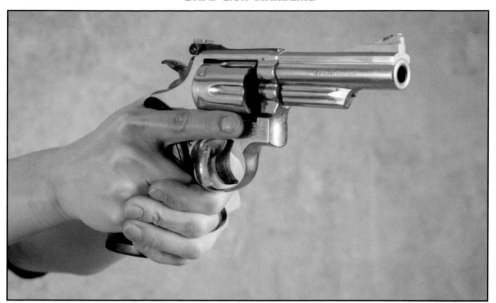

Most revolvers do not have a manual safety. Therefore, the user must rely on the NRA Three Gun Safety Rules. Note the application of NRA Rule #2: ALWAYS keep your finger off the trigger until ready to shoot.

When a shooter has made a conscious decision to shoot, he may place his finger on the trigger.

applying this knowledge. In both of these cases, accidents can easily happen. But when people practice responsible ownership and use of guns, accidents don't happen.

Though there are many specific principles of safe firearm operation, all are derived from just three basic safe gun handling rules.

ALWAYS keep the gun pointed in a safe direction. This is the primary rule of gun safety. A safe direction means that the gun is pointed so that even if it were to go off, it would not cause injury or damage. The key to this rule is to control where the muzzle or front end of the barrel is pointed at all times. Common sense dictates the safest direction, depending upon the circumstances. At the range, a "safe direction" is downrange. If only this one safety rule were always followed, there would be no injuries or damage from unintentional discharges.

Keeping a firearm pointed in a safe direction is relatively easy with a long gun, such as a rifle or shotgun, as the longer barrel promotes muzzle awareness. The shorter length of the typical revolver or semi-automatic, and its ability to be held and fired in one hand, require that the shooter be even more conscious of where the gun is pointing.

ALWAYS keep your finger off the trigger until ready to shoot. Your trigger finger should always be kept straight, alongside the frame and out of the trigger guard, until you have made the decision to shoot. Unintentional discharges can be caused when the trigger of a loaded gun is inadvertently pressed by a finger left in the trigger

Shooter demonstrating the proper way to carry a rifle that has a two-point sling. In this case the shooter is pointing it in the safest direction (downrange), and should have its action open.

Proper range etiquette and safety for firearms laying on a table proscribe that they are pointed in a safe direction (downrange), and should have their actions open.

guard instead of being positioned straight along the side of the gun's frame.

ALWAYS keep the gun unloaded until ready to use. A firearm that is not being used should always be unloaded. For example, at the range, your firearm should be left unloaded with the action open while you walk down-range to check your target. Similarly, a firearm that is stored in a gun safe or lock box should be unloaded (unless it is a personal protection firearm that may need to be accessed quickly for defensive purposes).

As a general rule, whenever you pick up a gun, point it in a safe direction with your finger off the trigger, engage the safety (if the gun is equipped with one), remove the magazine (if the gun is equipped with a removable magazine), open the action, and visually and physically inspect the chamber(s) to determine if the gun is loaded or not. Unless the firearm is being kept in a state of readiness for personal protection, it should be unloaded. If you do not know how to open the action or inspect the firearm, leave the gun alone and get help from someone who does.

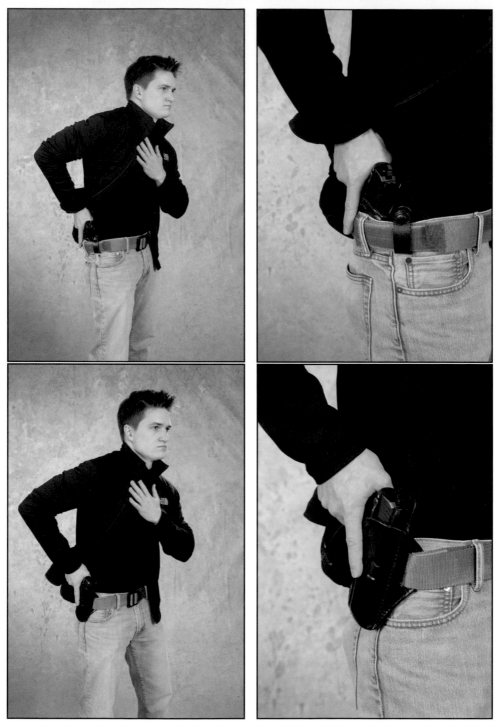

The photographs above and on the next page show how to properly pull a firearm from a belt holster. Access and grip the gun; make sure you have a solid grip before pulling your gun from the holster, with your trigger finger held straight.

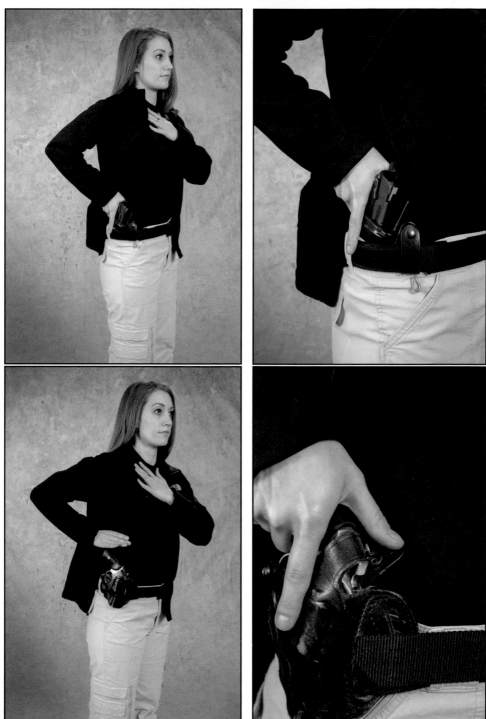

As you push down to grip your gun, keep your thumb stiff to release the holster's thumb safely.

Rules for Using or Storing a Gun

In addition to these three fundamental Rules for Safe Gun Handling, you need to observe a number of additional rules when you use or store your firearm.

Know your target and what is beyond. Whether you are at the range, in the woods, or in a self-defense situation, if you're going to shoot, you must know what lies beyond your target. In almost all cases, you must be sure that there is something that will serve as a backstop to capture bullets that miss or go through the target. Even in an emergency, you must never fire in a direction in which there are innocent people or any other potential for mishap. Think first, shoot second.

Know how to use the gun safely. Before handling a gun, learn how it operates. Read the Owner's Manual for your gun. Contact the gun's manufacturer for an Owner's Manual if you do not have one. Know your gun's basic parts, how to safely open and close the action, and how to remove ammunition from the gun. No matter how much you know about guns, you must always take the time to learn the proper way to operate any new or unfamiliar firearm. Never assume that because one gun resembles another, they both operate similarly.

Modern semi-automatic pistols have levers, buttons, and switches. Learning the proper controls and what they are for is imperative for the safe use of your firearm. If you do not have the owner's manual for your firearm, contact the manufacturer to obtain one.

Also, remember that a gun's mechanical safety is never foolproof. Guidance in safe gun operation should be obtained from the owner's manual or a qualified firearm instructor or gunsmith. Knowing how to use the gun safely is especially important with pistols, as there is a multitude of different types of pistol mechanisms, each with its own specific operating procedure. Most long guns of a particular type (such as bolt-action rifles or pump-action shotguns) work in essentially the same way, allowing an individual familiar with one model to be likely to know how to operate another of the same type. This cannot always be said of pistols, particularly semi-automatic pistols.

Be sure your gun is safe to operate. Just like other tools, guns need regular maintenance. Proper cleaning and storage are part of the gun's general upkeep. If there is any question regarding a gun's ability to function, it should be examined by a knowledgeable gunsmith. Proper maintenance procedures are found in your owner's manual.

Use only the correct ammunition for your gun. Each firearm is intended for use with a specific cartridge. Only cartridges designed for a particular gun can be fired safely in that gun. Most guns have the ammunition type stamped on the barrel and/or slide. The owner's manual will also list the cartridge or cartridges appropriate for your gun. Ammunition can be identified by information printed on the cartridge box and usually stamped on the cartridge head. Do not shoot the gun unless you absolutely know you have the proper ammunition.

Using only the correct ammunition for your gun is of special importance with pistols, as there are some pistol cartridges that have several names. Moreover, there are a number of different cartridges which have the same external dimensions, and thus fit in the same firearm chamber, but produce strikingly different operating pressures. Furthermore, even for the same cartridge there may be loadings having varying levels of pressure and performance. These higher pressure loads must be used only in a firearm designed for them.

Wear eye and ear protection as appropriate. The sound of a gunshot can damage unprotected ears. Gun discharges can also emit debris and hot gas that could cause eye injury. Thus, both ear and eye protection are highly recommended whenever you are firing live ammunition in your gun. Safety glasses and ear plugs or muffs should also be worn by any spectators or shooting partners present during live-fire sessions.

Never use alcohol or drugs before or while shooting. Alcohol and many drugs can impair normal mental and physical bodily functions, sharply diminishing your ability to use a gun safely. These substances must never be used before or while handling or shooting guns.

Note that these effects are produced not just by illegal or prescription drugs. Many over-the-counter medications also have considerable side effects which may be multiplied when certain drugs are taken together or with alcohol.

Inspect the head stamp of the cartridge to ensure you are using the correct ammunition for your gun.

Read the label of any medication you take, even common non-prescription medications, or consult your physician or pharmacist for possible side effects. If the label advises against driving or operating equipment while taking the medication, you should also avoid using a firearm while taking it.

Store guns so they are inaccessible to unauthorized persons. It is your responsibility as a gun owner to take reasonable steps to prevent unauthorized persons (especially children) from handling or otherwise having access to your firearms.

Be aware that certain types of guns and many shooting activities require additional safety precautions. There are many different types of firearms, some of which require additional safety rules or procedures for proper operation. These are commonly found in your firearm's owner's manual. Also, most sport shooting activities have developed sets of rules to ensure safety during competition. These rules are generally sport-specific; the procedures for loading your firearm and commencing fire, for example, are different in NRA Bullseye Shooting than in NRA Action Pistol Competition.

Special Responsibilities for Parents

Parents should be aware that a child could discover a gun when a responsible adult is not present. This situation could occur in the child's own home, the home of a neighbor, friend, or relative, or in a public place (such as a park). To avoid the possibility of an accident in such a situation, the child should be taught to apply the following gun safety rules if he or she sees a gun:

Stop!
Don't Touch.
Run Away.
Tell a Grownup.

This message is part of a special accident-prevention program known as the Eddie Eagle GunSafe Program. Developed by the NRA for young children (pre-kindergarten through fourth grade), it uses the friendly character of Eddie Eagle to teach children to follow Eddie's four rules.

Avoid Getting Scoped

For most centerfire rifle calibers, three to five inches is the recommended distance from your eye to the scope; a scope with about four inches of eye relief will be very safe. This longer eye relief is necessary to keep the scope from hitting the shooter's eyebrow when the rifle recoils. Pay particular attention to the eye-relief specification when buying a scope for a magnum rifle. High-magnification scopes tend to have less eye relief, as do variable power scopes. Economy scopes also tend to scrimp on eye relief. Handgun scopes are normally fired at arm's length, and require a scope with extra-long eye relief (in excess of twenty inches).

Bolt-Action Rifle

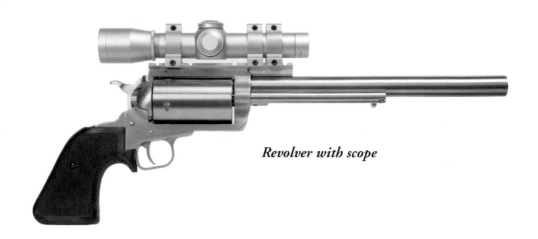

Revolver with scope

Bolt-Action Rifle

Pro-Hunter

Revolvers

Unless you are using a speedloader or speedstrip, a double-action revolver loads a single cartridge by hand into one chamber at a time. It is a slow process compared to inserting a fully loaded magazine into a semi-automatic pistol. Older single-action revolvers are typically loaded with only five cartridges with the hammer down on the empty chamber. Modern single-actions have transfer-bar safety systems that allows the hammer to be left in the down position so that all chambers maybe loaded.

Generally, speedloaders are capable of loading all chambers of a revolver simultaneously, and speedloaders are also marketed for the loading of the fixed tubular magazines of some shotguns and rifles, or even loading a box or drum magazine. Revolver speedloaders can be used for guns with either swing-out or top-break cylinders, but older-style revolvers having fixed cylinders, and a swing-out loading gate must be unloaded and loaded one chamber at a time.

Loading slowly and purposefully can be seen as a form of enforced safety because the revolver will not fire unless the active cylinder is loaded with a live round and then closed.

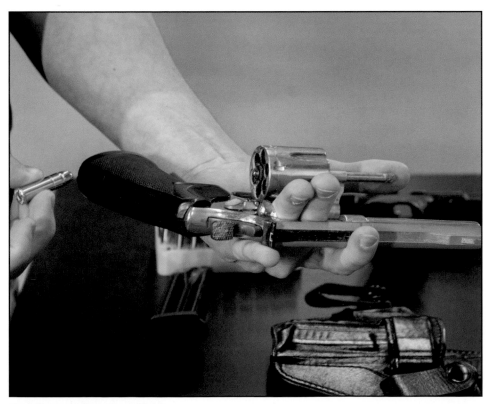

Revolver with open cylinder

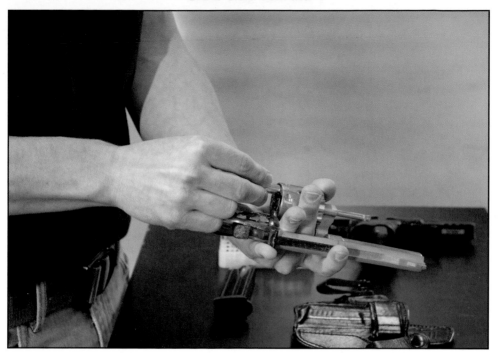

Individually inserting one cartridge into one of the chambers.

Fully loaded cylinder

On most revolvers with swing-out-type cylinders, press cylinder release latch with right thumb to access the chamber.

Swing out cylinder by pressing cylinder out with two fingers.

To remove empty or unfired cartridges, cradle the gun with the left hand, then press the ejector rod (left thumb backwards).

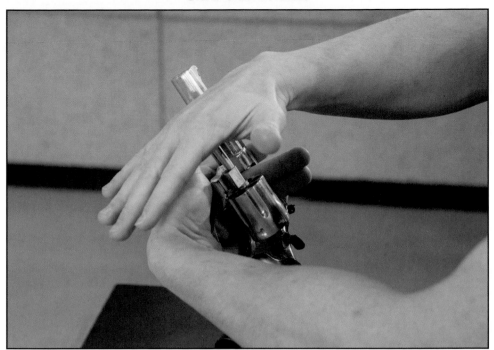

Alternatively the user may tap the ejector rod with the right hand while cradling the revolver with the left hand.

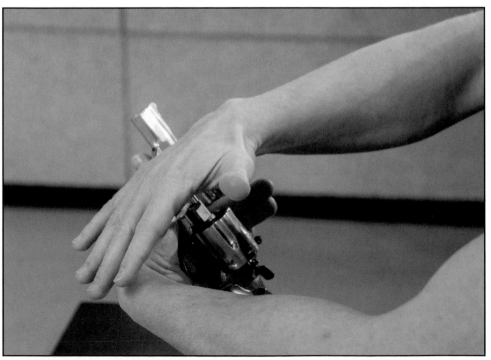

Let the empty casings fall to the gound.

Semi-Automatic Pistols

A semi-automatic pistol magazine typically has four components: magazine body, spring, floor plate, and a follower. Semi-automatic pistol magazines, when loaded by hand, are loaded by inserting one cartridge onto the follower of a magazine compressing the spring inside the magazine. The first couple of cartridges are easy but become progressively more difficult as the cartridges compress the spring inside the magazine. Reloading a semi-automatic pistol may be done very quickly. Press the magazine release button, and insert a loaded magazine into the magazine well of the pistol. After the magazine is inserted in the pistol, give the floor plate of the magazine a slight pull to make sure it is fully seated, and then release the slide. To release the slide the user may press the slide release lever, or pull the slide back with the non-shooting hand releasing the slide forward.

Always wear ear and eye protection.

Unload the chamber.

Visually check the chamber.

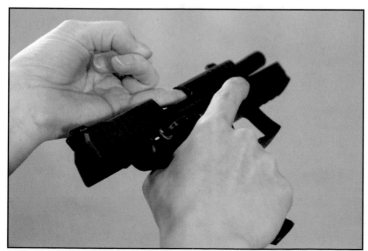

Ensure the chamber is clear of ammunition obstructions.

To load a semi-automatic magazine, place the back of the cartridge onto the follower inside the magazine or on top of the previous cartridge. (Note: You must place it into the wider part of the top of the magazine, or you will not be able to push it through the narrow top of the magazine body.)

Compress the magazine spring by pressing the cartridge down into the magazine.

Once you have loaded the magazine with the desired number of cartridges, insert the magazine into the bottom of the pistol untill it is firmly seated. (Note: The bullet component of the cartidge should be facing away from you.)

You can release the slide forward into "battery" by pulling the slide to the read and letting it spring forward on its own. (Note: Once you pull the slide back do not keep your hand on it, let it spring forward on its own!) Alternatively, if your pistol has a slide lock/release lever, you can depress the lever to let the slide spring forward on its own.

Pump-Action Shotguns

When picking up a pump-action, make sure the safety is on, the chamber unloaded, and the barrel pointed in a safe direction. Use only the correct size shotgun shell. Loading is easier if you first find a stable position for the butt of the stock. Place the butt on your thigh or hip and secure the stock under your arm with the gun turned sideways. Place a single shotgun shell against the lifter just ahead of the trigger guard. The shell is designed to fit only one way; don't force it. The non-metallic crimped end points toward the muzzle. Using your thumb, push the shotgun shell against the magazine follower up into the tube located underneath the barrel until it clicks. This means the rim of the shell should have passed the magazine catch. Repeat until the magazine tube is full. The tube will be full when you are unable to load another shell. To load a shotgun shell into the chamber, press the action release button (usually located around the trigger guard) and pump the slide backward and then forward with a reasonable amount of force. Sliding the pump-action backward will open the action, remove a shotgun shell from the tube, and place it on the lifter. Sliding the pump forward will insert it into the chamber. The shotgun is now ready to fire. Another way to load the pump-action shotgun is to slide the pump to the rear, place a shotgun shell through the ejection port resting it on the lifter, then slide the pump forward. The shooter may then load the shotgun's tube to its capacity.

With the shotgun facing a safe direction and your finger off the trigger, open the action of the semi-automatic shotgun. This is accomplished by pulling back the charging handle to the rear. (Note: Some shotguns require you to activate a switch, which will lock the bolt to the rear. Check your owner's manual for this information.)

Insert the cartridge on the lifter by placing it through the ejection port with the primer of the shotgun shell facing the rear.

Release the bolt by pressing the bolt release (check owner's manual for location of the bolt release).

With the non-shooting hand, insert shotgun shells into the tube of the shotgun underneath the barrel.

Push the shell against the lifter and slide it into the tube until you hear an audible click. (Note: Most new shotguns will only allow you to load two shells into the magazine tube due to an ammunition restrictor plug placed in the tube factory. This plug is required by federal regulations for hunting migratory birds and waterfowl. Check your local state and federal laws before you remove it.)

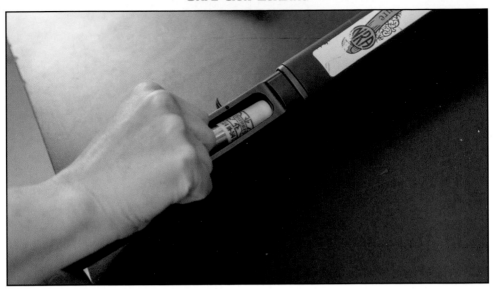

Underside view sliding shotgun shell into magazine tube

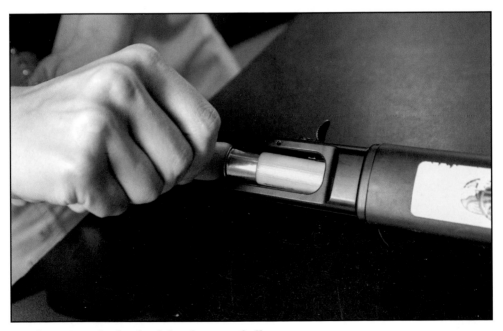

Push against the back of the shotgun shell.

Semi-Automatic Shotguns

A semi-automatic (self-loading) shotgun loads similar to a pump. The first shell can be loaded directly through the ejection port, after which you push the bolt release to close the bolt and chamber the shell. Additional shotgun shells can be pushed into the tubular magazine with your thumb until it is full.

Unload a pump or semi-auto by pushing the lifter down and removing the shells by hand. To remove a chambered shell, simply work the action by hand.

Hinge-Action Shotgun

A hinge-action, popularly known as a "break-action," side-by-side, or over/under shotgun, is simple because there is no magazine tube to load. First, engage the mechanical safety if applicable, then locate the action release lever, latch, or button. The gun opens at a hinge so you can load a shell directly into the chamber of the barrel (or barrels). A hinge-action gun must be reloaded after every shot (or every two shots if you have a double-barreled gun). Open the hinge-action and lower the barrel away from the body of the shotgun. Remove and discard the spent casings with care, as they may be hot if the gun was recently fired. Replace the used casings with fresh shotgun shells and bring the barrel back up to close the action until it clicks. The shotgun is now ready to fire.

You can shoot smaller shells in some larger-gauge shotguns: 20-, 28-, or .410 gauge in a 12-gauge, for example. However this requires the use of specialty tubes. Briley, for example, builds its Companion Drop-In tube sets for side-by-sides and over/under shotguns. Tubes are brand-specific, but simply slip into and out of the barrel. The weight of a standard set of 20-gauge Briley Companions varies by barrel length and bore size.

Bolt-Action Rifles

For many years, the bolt-action rifle has been the standard for hunters and competitors. To load and fire the bolt-action rifle, first engage the mechanical safety if applicable, then you will need remove any ammunition source. For bolt-actions that have a removable box magazine, remove the magazine using the magazine release lever similar to a semi-automatic pistol. Bolt-action rifles with a hinged floor plate (metal plate usually found in front of the trigger guard) will need to be opened and checked first for live ammunition. Locate the floor plate release button, and then press the button to open the floor plate releasing any ammunition in the magazine of the rifle.

To check for ammunition in an internal bolt-action rifle, empty the magazine by releaseing the floor plate, located on the bottom of the gun. If your gun does not have a hinged floor plate you will first need to pull the bolt rearward until the cartridge in change ejects. (Note: Check your owner's manual for the hinged floor plate operation.)

To load most bolt-action rifles that do not have a hinged floor plate or external magazine, you will need to load from the top of the action. Simply insert a cartridge into the follower and press it into the internal magazine.

Once the desired number of cartridges are in the internal magazine, close the bolt by pushing it forward.

Push bolt downwards to lock the bolt into place.

The gun is now loaded and ready to fire.

Once you have removed the ammunition source, pull the bolt handle up and back, opening the action. (Don't force it; it should come easily.) Check for and remove any remaining cartridges in the breech.

Once empty, locate a loaded magazine, place it below the magazine well under the stock, and push it in until it clicks. Rifles with an internal magazine or hinged floor plate require manual loading by placing the cartridge round on the magazine follower and pressing it into the internal magazine located behind the breech until it is secure. Some rifles may use a stripper clip which will load a number of cartridges at one time into the internal magazine. Such rifles typically take five to ten rounds.

Push the bolt forward as far as you can, and then push it down to close it. The bolt head is designed so that it strips a cartridge from the top of the magazine and pushes it into the chamber. The rifle is now ready to fire.

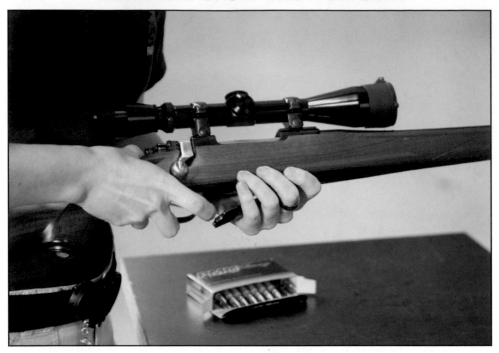

To unload the gun, first remove the ammunition source. Open the hinge floor plate located on the bottom of the rifle in front of the trigger guard.

Slowly allow ammunition to be released from the internal magazine.

Pull the bolt rearward until cartridge in chamber ejects. Then visually and physically inspect the chamber.

Once ammunition is released, pull bolt up.

Semi-Automatic Rifles

Semi-automatic rifle magazines typically have four components similar to a pistol magazine. Semi-automatic rifle magazines, when loaded by hand, are loaded by inserting one cartridge onto the follower of a magazine, compressing the spring inside the magazine. Most rifle magazines are loaded by lining up the cartridge and length of the magazine and simple pressing down through the magazine body feed lips. Reloading a semi-automatic rifle may be done very quickly, similarly to the semi-automatic pistol. Press the magazine release button, and insert a loaded magazine into magazine well of the rifle. After the magazine is inserted in the rifle, give the magazine body a slight pull to ensure it is seated properly, and then release the bolt slide. To release the bolt, the shooter may press the bolt release lever or pull the charging handle back with the non-shooting hand, releasing the bolt forward.

With a staggered box magazine for a rifle, place top cartridge flush with the magazine and press straight down into the magazine.

Repeat until magazine is filled to capacity or desired number of cartridges.

For best support, place the buttstock of the rifle under the shooting arm. With your non-firing hand, "push" the magazine with the bullets facing forward into the magazine well until you hear an audible click.

Pull on the magazine until you feel that it's seated properly.

Press the bolt release to release the bolt.

The gun is now loaded and ready to shoot.

A Few Muzzleloader Notes

With the invention of the in-line muzzleloader, shooting muzzleloaders have gained in popularity with both recreational shooters and hunters. However, traditional cap and ball and flintlock muzzleloaders are still popular among traditionalists, and in part some states requiring them as per state law for the primitive muzzleloading hunting season.

First, make sure the gun is not "primed," which means no cap on the nipple of a percussion gun and no priming powder in the pan of a flintlock. Make sure the bore is clean of fouling and oil by running a dry patch down the bore. (Some fouling is normal with these black-powder guns.) After using a patch, shooters should fire a few percussion caps or a few pans of powder at a blade of grass to ensure it moves, which indicates the primer hole is open and functioning properly.

With the gun propped up in a safe place where it's stable and won't fall over, such as between the shooter's legs or in the corner of a shooting bench, set your powder measure for the desired powder charge. Pour the powder from the measure (not like Davy Crockett, directly from a cow horn or flask) into the muzzle. Tap the butt against the ground or the heel of your hand against the barrel to help settle the powder.

To load a patched round ball, place a lubricated cloth patch over the end of the barrel. Center the ball on the patch. If the ball has a sprue or mold mark, center the mark and face upward.

To load a maxi-ball or other conical bullet, first make sure you have lubricated it to the bullet manufacturer's specifications. Place the bullet on the muzzle and start pushing it down by hand. Once the ball is as far as it will go, use your bullet starter to push the projectile slightly into the bore using the short portion of your starter. Next, if you have a longer section on your starter, push the bullet into the bore as far as your starter will allow.

Using your ramrod, shove the projectile down the bore until it contacts the powder charge. Seat each bullet firmly, with as close to the same pressure as you can manage. You may want to mark your ramrod and use the mark to ensure that each load is seated to the same depth. Do not fire a muzzleloader unless the projectile is seated firmly against the powder charge.

Now, prime your muzzleloader. For percussion models, cock the hammer and place a properly sized percussion cap onto the nipple. Carefully hold the hammer back with your thumb and pull the trigger; now gently lower the hammer until it almost touches the cap. Release the trigger while still holding the hammer, and pull the hammer back until it clicks one time. This should place your gun at the half-cock (safety position).

For flintlocks, open the frizzen and pour a small amount of Goex FFg Black

Pour powder into powder measure.

Pour powders into barrel.

Patch ball using short starter.

Trim patch.

Prime pan

Ramrod to push bullet down barrel.

Powder into the pan, about enough powder to half-fill the depression in the pan. Place your gun at half-cock, making sure you don't allow the flint to create any sparks.

To ready it for firing, fully cock the hammer until it clicks into the full-cock position. The gun is now ready to fire. It should not be cocked until it is pointed at an appropriate target.

A couple notes about muzzleloaders and black powder: Never fire a muzzleloader unless the projectile is seated firmly against the powder charge. Doing so could cause serious bodily harm and or death to the user or bystanders.

If you forget the powder, use a bullet puller (worm), a sharp screw that fits on the end of your ramrod, to attempt to remove the bullet. The easiest way to remove a bullet inside a barrel is with a special device that fits over the nipple of the muzzleloader, powering the device is a twelve gram CO_2 container that will safely push the bullet out. Another possible way to remove a bullet in the barrel is to pour a little powder into the barrel through the priming hole. For flintlocks, look for a

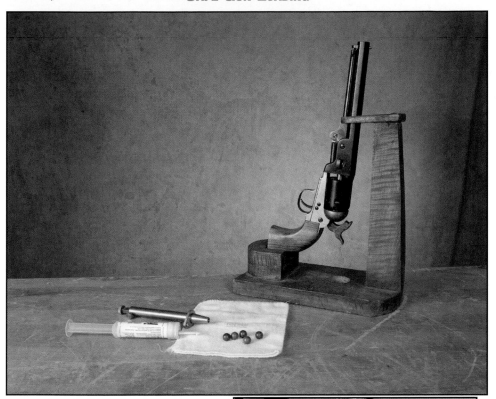

Pistol loading stand

screw that will allow you to pour powder into the chamber. Then replace the nipple or screw and use your ramrod to seat the bullet all the way down. Prime your firearm and shoot the bullet clear. Use your ramrod to check and make sure that the bullet was fully driven out of the bore and that the barrel is completely clear. If it is not, use a bullet puller, or repeat the process, once again making sure to ram the projectile all the way down each time you attempt to shoot it out of the barrel. If you can't ram the ball down the bore, then you must either use a bullet puller to remove it, or disassemble the gun and push the bullet out through the muzzle.

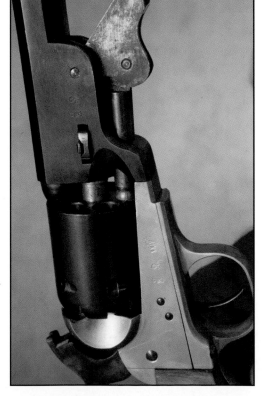

Put ball into chamber of cylinder.

Push ball into chamber.

Reloading—Handloading

As you begin your adventure into shooting, you will encounter plenty of people who make their own ammunition. It is a relatively inexpensive hobby called reloading or handloading. Essentially it allows you to recycle ammo for your firearms by assembling the individual components (case/hull, primer, powder, and bullet/shot) rather than purchasing factory-loaded ammunition. By following a few guidelines, it is safe and completely fascinating.

The essential ingredients are time, patience, and an ability to follow directions. You can find those instructions through the NRA or at your local gun club. You do not need anyone looking over your shoulder when you are measuring

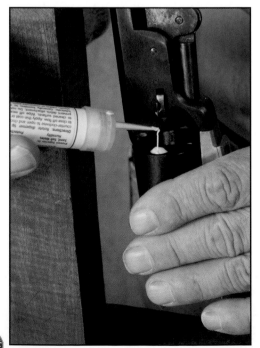

powder or seating a bullet. In this regard, handloading is like hunting; you may choose to enjoy this niche in the shooting sports entirely on your own.

Why would someone want to go through the process of building their own shells or cartridges when it is so easy to purchase them at a local sporting goods or big-box store?

1. The last few years have shown that not all loads and sizes are readily available (like the recent ammunition shortage) and when they are, there are various grades of advertised commercial ammunition.

Use bore butter or Crisco to prevent chain firing.

The premium or perhaps inexpensive grade that you prefer may well be out of stock.

2. There are cost savings. If you shoot frequently, you may be able to manufacture cartridges for half the retail price after acquiring the initial equipment.

Pour powder into chamber from powder measure.

3. Building your own loads allows you to experiment and customize loads for your gun and a variety of shooting situations. What you shoot on the trap range may not be what you want to take pheasant hunting.

4. Handloading is fun. It is a quiet science. It does not require a PhD to participate, only patience and the ability to read and carefully follow directions.

Getting Started

You can handload for almost any gun, any caliber or gauge, and while there is equipment to purchase and learn to use, this is not an expensive hobby. Here are a few of the items you will need. Just remember that a class teaching the fundamentals along with an experienced mentor will take most of the nervousness out of the process. The same can be said for following traditional "recipes," the directions for building a load. Today, instead of shopping for each item separately, reloading-materials manufacturers often sell complete sets of gear—one-stop shopping.

- A mechanical press. A commercial press can be purchased to load almost any centerfire cartridge ever invented. Presses are also available for reloading shotshells. Begin with an inexpensive single-stage press that includes a shellplate or shellholder and performs one operation at a time. It allows you to load fifty to sixty cases/hulls an hour. So if you shoot only two hundred rounds a month for example, a single stage is sufficient. If and when you are hooked on reloading, step up to a faster (sometimes much faster), but more expensive progressive press that performs multiple operations and generates a shell or cartridge each time you pull the handle. A press is easy to operate and requires little maintenance.

- For centerfire cartridges you will need a set of dies. The dies go into the press and do the actual work on the cartridge case. Dies

Reloading press

come as sets that are cartridge specific. Depending on your setup, dies remove the spent primer, resize the case and expand the throat area for a new bullet, seat the new bullet in the case, and crimp it into place.

- You will need reloading data, a set of recipes explaining what type of ingredient and how much you should use. The best sources are reloading manuals published by bullet and powder manufacturers. Most contain data for a number of different cartridges, some history of the cartridges, and tips for loading effective rounds. Some manuals are free and others can be downloaded from a manufacturer's website.

- It is important to purchase a good reloading scale that is calibrated in grains so you can check the weight of your charge, weight of bullets or shot, and calibrate your powder measure if it is adjustable.

As your interest develops you may accumulate an incredible set of tools: a dial caliper to measure cases (especially necessary for semi-automatic handguns, which can be finicky about reloads), a case trimmer to make sure all cases are the same precise length, a deburring tool to smooth up the trimmed area, and perhaps a case tumbler/vibrator to clean used cases. Soon you will want a chronograph to measure the velocity of your hand-loaded bullets (despite their electronics, chronographs are not that expensive).

Once you develop an interest and begin to assemble the tools, you will need components—powders, cases, shot or bullets, primers, and all the other premium ingredients that make for a fine handload.

Before packages begin arriving at your home, give a great deal of thought to where you will take on the reloading. Ideally it will be a dedicated space. After all, you have powders that can burn and contain hazardous ingredients. The kitchen table may be the ideal place to clean an empty firearm, but it may not be ideal for reloading unless you live alone.

You can bolt a single stage press to a sturdy piece of wood and clamp to any stable surface to reload. This provides a portable unit that will not be in the way when it goes used. As you progress in reloading, though, and acquire larger presses, you will need a dedicated area and sturdy bench to permanently mount your press.

The place you decide to reload on a more permanent basis must have:

- A secure and lockable door to keep out intruders and minimize interruptions. Reloading should take place in an area where you can concentrate without being disturbed.

- A room in which you can control dust, temperature, and humidity to protect the sensitive components.

Safety Considerations

Reloading ranks far below children's toys as a source of accidental injury. Overall it's a remarkably safe hobby. The potential for accidents is inherent in the person doing the work and not in the hobby, equipment, or materials. In the end, you are your own margin of safety. After all, an improperly or poorly constructed cartridge can either fail to fire or fire prematurely or even blow up in the barrel if the recipe is not stringently followed. Safety equals fun.

Use a reloading manual or tested formulas from a reputable source and follow the directions to the letter. Do not substitute or interchange ingredients unless your manual specifically allows it. Substituting a fast-burning powder in a load designed for a slow-burning powder will cause problems. Never mix powders or use unidentified powders. Don't guess and don't try to identify gunpowder by its physical appearance. Not even an expert can do that. The one and only acceptable identification of a powder is the factory label on its original container, not in a cartridge case and not in an unlabeled canister. If the latter happens as a result of violations of other safety rules, destroy the resultant mixture.

Do not attempt to extrapolate a new burning rate for the mix and use it; relative quickness is not all that simple.

Watch for signs of high pressure while working up a rifle or pistol handload. This means extraction difficulty (however slight), flattened primers, cratered primers, ironed-out headstamps, polished headstamps, ejector marks, case-head expansion, and excessive recoil and muzzle blast . . . plus anything else that strikes you as abnormal about the load.

As you begin to learn reloading for your chosen cartridge, start low and work up. Don't begin with the maximum charge possible and never exceed the maximum charge allowed. Never deviate from published recipes when loading shotshells. Use only the exact materials and quantities specified for a shotshell load.

Hornady unprimed brass cases

Carefully examine and select every hull or case. Discard any that appear worn, or show cracks or any other defect. Trying to squeeze just one more shot out of weakened brass has spelled catastrophe for more than one reloader.

Don't be in a hurry. Reload carefully and accurately. Loading in a hurry can mean an inaccurate setting on a powder scale or using the wrong powder. At best, haste defeats the whole purpose of reloading, which is superior ammunition for your guns. At worst, haste can result in disaster.

Avoid distractions while reloading. That means never smoking while reloading. No watching a football game while reloading. Don't invite over friends or carry on a bull session while stuffing powder and shot. Reloading is a relatively precise activity and mistakes can be serious. It is also a superb idea to refrain from drinking until your reloading day is done.

To guard against mistakes, develop a reloading routine. Form procedures at the loading bench to establish well-thought-out habits and avoid slipshod ones. This rule really applies as much to shooting your handloads as to building them. For example, a personal rule of never having more than one ammunition box open on the shooting bench at one time may prevent your trying to fire the wrong cartridge in a gun.

As far as ingredients and processes are concerned, here are a few safety tips that will keep you out of trouble.

1. Always check powder and shot charges with a reliable scale.

2. Store primers in their original factory trays in a cool, dry area, as primers are flammable and capable of exploding.

3. Store powder in a dark, cool, dry area; out of children's reach; away from open fire or heat. Powder, too, is flammable. Store your powders in small quantities in approved containers, away from such combustibles as solvents, inflammable gases, and of course open flame.

4. Wear eye protection while reloading.

5. Keep your reloading area clean and neat. Reloading involves hazardous materials, including lead. Wash your hands before and after reloading.

6. Never shoot without approved safety glasses and hearing protection.

A few final thoughts about components:

- Bullets and Shot. Be sure that they are the recommended diameter and weight. Keep bullet calibers and weights in separate and accurately marked containers. Do not mix or interchange bullets from various manufacturers in the same reloading formula. And don't substitute calibers, use only that for which your gun is chambered exactly (a .300 Winchester Magnum for example is not a .300 Weatherby Magnum). Check the weight of charges thrown by your measure or bar to be sure it conforms to recipe recommendations.

- Primers. A primer is essentially a tiny explosion waiting to happen. It must be handled carefully without dropping, shaking, hammering on it, or heating, and stored in a cool, dry place. An exploding primer can cause others around it to explode because primers can explode simultaneously, it is generally recommended that when hand loading, primers should be handled individually and never subjected to undue force. Hand-loading equipment must be electrically grounded and the room should be clean and free of primer dust and powder buildup. If you spill a box of primers, pick them up immediately because they may explode if stepped on. Because chemicals like solvents, even water, may cause deterioration, your ammunition should be carefully segregated during gun cleaning.

  Primers are manufactured in different types and sizes, each designed to be used in specific cartridges. Do not substitute primer types, even if they will physically fit in your cartridge. An incorrect primer can result in your load having too much or too little pressure, neither of which is good.

  Store only in the original manufacturer's package. Keep a minimum amount on your loading bench. Remove unused primers from your loading tool after each session and return to the original package for storage. Do not store primers in bulk. Mass detonation may occur. Use only the brand of primers specified in the loading recommendations.

- Cases and Shells. Critical cartridge specifications include neck size, bullet weight and caliber, maximum pressure, headspace, overall length, case-body diameter and taper, shoulder design, and rim type. Do not mix brands, as case volume may be different, affecting loading density and pressure. Inspect for cracks, splits, stretch marks, separations, etc. after firing and before reloading. Do not load damaged or defective cases. Do not ream or enlarge primer flash holes. Examine fired shotshells for head damage, tube splits, pinholes, and basewad damage before reloading. Discard defective cases. Discard cases that show leakage around the primer or battery cup. Do not mix shotshells with high and low basewads. Do not mix brands of cases, as volumes may be different.

- Powder. Store in a cool, dry place in the original container in an approved storage cabinet. Keep container closed except when pouring. Never mix powders. Have only one specific type on your bench at one time to avoid unintentionally mixing powders. Keep a minimum amount of powder in the loading area. Don't use any powder when you are unsure of its identity. Don't mix or substitute powders of similar designations made by different companies. IMR 4350 is not the same powder as Hodgdon's H4350. Don't use any powder that appears discolored or is giving off fumes.

- Shotgun Wads. Use only the specific type listed in the recommendations. Do not mix or interchange types, as pressure levels can be affected.

Safety from SAAMI

The Sporting Arms and Ammunition Manufacturers' Institute (SAAMI) has compiled the following list of do's and don'ts for the handloader. Some of their rules repeat those given above, but information of this sort bears repeating because we're talking about avoiding some potentially serious accidents.

1. Follow only loading recommendations of a recognized current handloading guide. Better still, check two guides. Components and propellants change and old recommendations may be dangerous.
2. Don't use word-of-mouth loading data without checking a recognized current handloading guide.
3. Have the headspace of your firearm checked by a competent gunsmith at regular intervals, preferably by a factory-authorized repair station.
4. Examine fired cases for signs of excessive pressure, such as primer gas leaks, excessive primer flattening, loose primers, expanded heads or bodies, and side-wall stretching.
5. Investigate and determine the cause of any unusual or abnormal condition or appearance before continuing any operation.
6. Keep all components and loaded rounds positively identified.
7. Keep your work area and handloading bench scrupulously clean at all times. Immediately clean up any spillage of powder, primers, etc.
8. Do not chamber a round that resists easy closing of the bolt or action. The cartridge is too long or large in diameter and high pressure may develop.
9. Do not forget that a maximum load in your rifle may be dangerous in another one of your rifles or in a friend's rifle even if it is the same make, model, caliber, etc.
10. Components suitable for lead-shot loads are not adaptable to steel-shot loads.
11. The interchange of steel shot for lead results in dangerously high pressures that may damage shotguns. Ball bearings or steel air-rifle shot are not suitable for shotshell loads. They are much harder than steel shot.
12. Keep all components out of the reach of children.
13. Keep accurate, detailed records of all loads.
14. Don't load with charges that measure out to more than 10 percent below minimum recommendations.
15. Cartridge cases should be clean and dry before reloading and before firing. Oily cases greatly increase thrust against the bolt face.
16. Do not fireform factory cartridges in lengthened chambers. The excessive headspace is likely to be dangerous.
17. Be extremely careful to identify properly wildcat cases since the headstamp does not identify the new cartridge, which may have a larger diameter bullet than the original cartridge.
18. Do not use too much heat to dry cases to avoid softening the brass.
19. Do not use brass cases that have been in or near a fire.

Winchester Primers

*Lee 000
Buckshot
18 Mold*

Hornady Lock-N-Load Ammo Concentricity Tool

12-Gauge Remington STS 1X Hulls

Lee Load-All II 12-Gauge Shotshell Press

With the ever-growing development of our open lands we find that the days out in the field with Granddad throwing us a few clay targets for practice exist only in our memories. Today we head for the local ranges that are a more organized form of the shooting sports. Though ranges are sometimes a very busy place as our sport is growing in popularity, it is still very safe and fun for all ages. Shooting ranges are an excellent place to meet others who share your passion for the shooting sports. A shooting range or firing range is a specialized facility designed specifically for firearms practice. Some are built with public funding while others are private. Private ranges usually require membership of some sort. Shooting ranges can be indoor or outdoor and may restrict certain types of firearms, handguns-only for example. (There are even ranges dedicated strictly to archery.) A shotgun range may also specialize in specific shotgun games such as trap, skeet, or sporting clays.

Range safety is a cooperative function. To ensure range safety there should be strong leadership and all staff and visitors follow the range rules, which should be posted in various locations for all to see. Each facility is typically overseen by supervisory personnel such as Range Masters or Range Safety Officers. These folks are responsible for ensuring that safety rules are followed at all times. After all, "Safety is no accident. It must be planned and practiced."

A range-shooting safety plan must be clear and concise. But simply having a well-written document spelling out safety rules and regulations does not in itself create a safe environment. A properly designed and constructed physical plant alone—good barriers for sound and shot, a nice clubhouse, a parking area without ruts and excessive dust—does not guarantee a risk-free operation. No place in the world is "risk-free," but a shooting range with conscientious members and guests who understand and respect the rules may be one of the safest places in America.

Shooting Range Rules

1. Always keep the gun pointed in a safe direction.

2. Always keep your finger off the trigger until ready to shoot.

3. Always keep the gun unloaded until ready to use.

4. Know your target and what is beyond; make sure the downrange area is unoccupied.

5. Know how to use the gun safely.

6. Be sure the gun is safe to operate.

7. Use only the correct ammunition for your gun.

8. Wear eye and ear protection as appropriate.

9. Never use alcohol or drugs before or while shooting.

10. Unattended guns should not be accessible to unauthorized persons.

General Tips for Gun Range Safety

The following assumptions are the basis of a good range safety plan. The term "safe range" means all shots are fired in the direction of the targets; that users keep firearms unloaded and actions open when arriving or departing; that firearms are unloaded except when shooters are ready on the firing line; that users handle only firearms with which they are familiar and will always use the proper ammunition.

Handgun shooting at an indoor range.

Enforcement of the rules ties the separate parts into a cohesive and workable safety plan. Remember, a range is only as safe as the manner in which it is used and operated. You must obey all posted rules and regulations (even when nobody is looking), and conduct yourself in a responsible manner. Gun ownership may be a right, but shooting at the range is a privilege.

Gun-handling rules are of primary importance at every range, inside and outside. They should always appear first in a range safety plan and are prominently displayed at several locations throughout the range. As a minimum, the following rules (repeated elsewhere in this book) are critical to safe and continuous enjoyment of a day at the range:

• <u>ALWAYS</u> keep the gun pointed in a safe direction.
• <u>ALWAYS</u> keep your finger off the trigger until ready to shoot.
• <u>ALWAYS</u> keep the firearm unloaded until you are ready to shoot.
• Know how your firearm operates and what the range procedures are for a mechanical (gun or cartridge) failure.
• Be sure the firearm and ammunition is compatible. Think about carrying only one gauge or caliber of ammunition when you are shooting. When at a shooting range with more than one firearm, use one at a time and when complete, store that firearm and its ammunition before using the next one.
• Understand what to do in case you are involved in or observe an accident.
• Be sure of the target and what lies beyond it. When at a shooting range, be mindful also of adjacent areas and act accordingly.

High-power rifle shooting targets

- Wear eye and ear protection when appropriate.
- Do not mix alcohol or drugs, prescription or otherwise, with shooting activities. If you are involved in an emotional situation elsewhere, compartmentalize your emotion, leave it outside the gate.
- Be ultimately aware that you are part of a shooting community and conduct yourself accordingly. Police your own actions and those of your shooting companions. in a polite manner.
- Obey all range commands.
- Know where others are at all times.
- Shoot only at authorized targets. (Never shoot, for instance, at the stray bird that flies over the trap range because such a shot may have unforeseen consequences.)
- If no range officer is present and you are shooting in a group, designate your own range safety officer.
- During a ceasefire, unload, open the action, remove the magazine, and ground or bench all firearms.
- Do not touch firearms or ammunition belonging to others without their permission.

The Shotgun Sports

Trap, skeet, and sporting clays are the three primary disciplines in shotgun clay shooting. Each shooting discipline can be enjoyed strictly for fun with friends, or you can participate in an organized tournament in which competition is strictly regulated by national and international organizations.

In trap, targets are launched away from the shooter from a "trap house," a single position in front of the shooting line. In skeet shooting, targets are launched from two side houses in paths that intersect in front of the shooter. Sporting clays, sometimes called "golf with a shotgun," involves a more complex course, often through woods or fields, with numerous launch points. Sporting clays may even involve a shot called a "running rabbit," in which a clay-pigeon thrower bounces a round disk along the ground. Each game has numerous variations.

Sportsmanlike conduct is not quite the same as safety, but the two go hand in hand at a crowded range. Such behavior encourages a thoughtful relationship to others and to your firearm. A range is no place for horseplay or practical jokes. In the same manner as alcohol, offensive language is a terrible mix with firearms. Not every shot will be perfect. Displays of aggressive behavior, or throwing hats or shells, have to be carefully managed for everyone's safety.

Trap

Trapshooting was developed in England in the late eighteenth century, in part to augment bird hunting and to provide a method of practice for bird hunters. At first, live pigeons were released from cages known as traps. Glass balls were thrown for targets until clay targets were developed that could withstand the force of a long throw, yet still shatter when hit by a shot. Even today a shooter will call for "a bird" or a pigeon, meaning the clay disk.

Shooter about to fire at clay bird.

101

American Trap Shooting

American trap fields consist of a single trap machine sixteen yards in front of the firing line. The machines oscillate on a 45-degree arc, 22.5 degrees to either side of center. They are thrown ten feet high at a distance of ten yards in front of the house, and travel about fifty yards around forty miles an hour.

American trapshooting competition takes three forms: singles, handicap, and double-target shooting. In all three the targets are thrown from one trap, using 12-gauge shotguns. In singles shooting, contestants fire from a series of five stations located sixteen yards behind the trap. At a signal from the contestant, the clay target is launched forward into the air, away from the firing line. In order to simulate the unpredictable flight patterns of birds, the targets are launched out of the trap at various angles and directions. The clay pigeon rises to a minimum height of about ten feet and, unless hit, continues to rise until it loses momentum and falls to the ground, about fifty yards from the trap house. Champions often hit two hundred out of two hundred targets. In trapshooting, contestants possessing advanced skills are given handicaps and must shoot from stations as far as twenty-seven yards behind the trap. The added distance, or handicap, enables trapshooters of average ability to compete on equal terms with experts. In doubles, the trap launches two clay pigeons into the air simultaneously in different directions and the shooter fires at both clays one at a time.

Today the Amateur Trapshooting Association is the governing body of organized US and Canadian trapshooting. In trapshooting, as in other shooting sports, certain etiquette is followed especially during competitions. The following are some basic guidelines to get you started:
• Be certain of your assigned field and that you are on the correct bank.
• Be prepared and ensure that you have all of your equipment with you before your squad's turn. This includes the more obvious objects such as your ammunition, gun, and shooting vest or pouch.
• When your squad is up, you should immediately take the field.
• Be attentive between rounds. Take only enough time to get a drink of water, get your next box of shells, check your equipment, take a relaxing breath, and head back out to the field. If you take too much time between rounds you will hinder the flow of the shoot, causing delays that affect the end of the day.
• Have access to a spare gun should you have a gun malfunction that cannot easily be corrected within minutes on the line.

Once you take the field, the lead-off shooter should ensure that the squad is ready to shoot. Don't assume everyone is prepared, and ask the trapper (clay-pigeon puller) if he is ready. Look down the line and get confirmation from your squad mates that they are ready. Look back at the trapper to check and make sure that he is properly situated. Then, you can call for a show bird (it shows the flight of the clay targets). After the show bird, load your gun and call for your first target. When preparing to shoot, you should take your shells out of your pouch or a vest. It is distracting to the shooters around you, and hinders the flow of the shoot, if you have to bend over and get a shell out of a box from the ground for every shot. Avoid unnecessary movement, such as excessive shuffling of your feet on the station. No mounting of your gun before it is your turn, or leaving of your station. With the exception of doubles, trap is a single-shot game, so load only one shell at a time.

Competitors are serious about their shooting. Don't talk while on the station. Talking distracts other shooters, and with voice-automated calls you may inadvertently throw targets, disrupting the current shooter's rhythm. When you call for the target, do it in a clear, strong voice. This is important to ensure that you get a good pull, especially if the field is not equipped with voice calls. Don't shout so loud that you can cause the field next to you to release targets.

When you have finished shooting your station, remain there until all squad members have completed their station, then rotate. When moving from station five to station one it is proper to rotate clockwise off the station, always keeping your firearm from pointing at your fellow shooters. Rotate behind the line and other shooters. When you have completed your round, check your score with the trapper, make sure it is correct before the squad leader signs the sheet and before you leave the field. If you are the squad leader it is polite to ask your squad mates if their scores are correct before you sign the sheet and proceed to the next field.

Skeet

Skeet shooting was invented by an American sportsman, Charles Davis of Massachusetts, who was an avid grouse hunter. His original course was a full circle with a radius of twenty-five yards, its circumference marked off like the face of a clock and a trap set at the twelve o'clock position. However, shooting in a circle caused obvious practicality and safety issues, and the game evolved into its current setup by 1923 when William H. Foster placed a second trap at the six o'clock position and thus cut the course in half. Foster quickly noticed the appeal of this kind of fast-action competition shooting and set out to make it

American Skeet Shooting

a national sport. During World War II, skeet was used in the American military to teach gunners the principle of leading and timing on a flying target.

Skeet is in some ways similar to trap, yet in others, much different. The essential rules of safety and good sportsmanship apply, especially when shooting in a competition. Be certain of which field you will be shooting on. Be prepared and ready to go before your turn is up. It is inconsiderate to be late, making your squad wait, and you should ensure that you have all of your equipment with you when you arrive at the field.

In skeet, the shooting process is different than in trap because the arrangement of the field is different. This means that safety depends on following a practical order. Do not load your gun, for instance, until you are on the station ready to shoot. When you have completed shooting at a station, make sure to completely remove the empty shells from your gun, and that your action is open before you leave the station. You may not move to the next station with a loaded gun. When you are not shooting make sure that your action is open, that your gun is unloaded, and that you are keeping the muzzle pointed in a safe direction.

When you have finished shooting your station, remain behind that station until all squad members have completed shooting, then you may rotate to the next station. When you move to the next station it is customary to line up in shooting order. This will help make transitioning on and off the station quicker. When you have completed your round, check your score with the puller, making sure it is correct before the squad leader signs the sheet and before you leave the field.

International Skeet

International skeet has had Olympic status since 1968. International skeet is very similar to American skeet in that the target comes out of two skeet houses, which are located on the left and right portions of the front of the field.   The difference is that there is a random delay between zero to three seconds after the shooter has called for the target. Targets come out of the skeet houses at about sixty-five miles per hour. The shooter must start from the low gun mount which means they hold the gun so that the buttstock is just above the hip at mid-torso level, marked by a yellow strip on the shooter's vest, and must remain there until the target appears. Another difference is the shooters shoot doubles, not only on stations 1, 2, 6, and 7, as in American skeet, but also on 3, 4, and 5. This includes a reverse double (low house first) on station 4.

International Trap

International trap, also known as "Bunker Trap," is another shotgun game that is featured in the Olympics. Clay targets come out of the bunker-like trap house, and can fly up to 110 mph. As in American trap there are five stations you shoot from, and international trap has three trap machines for each of the stations randomly throwing the targets when called for. Trap machines are set for angles up to 45 degrees right and left. The targets are set to a distance of 76 meters. Since there are so many variables, a shooter may shoot twice at each outgoing target even if he brakes the target on the first shot. They can shoot at pieces with their second shell. Doubles is the final shotgun event in the Olympics; it has been part of the Olympics since 1996. It is shot from the international trap field but only the three machines from station 3 are used. As the name would imply, when the shooter calls, two clays are launched.

Sporting Clays

Unlike trap and skeet, which are games of target presentations, sporting clays simulates the unpredictability of live-quarry shooting, offering a great variety of trajectories, angles, speeds, elevations, distances, and even target sizes. A typical sporting clays course includes ten to fifteen different shooting stations laid out over natural terrain that will add up to a fifty- or one-hundred- shot course. For safety, the course size is often no smaller than thirty-five acres.

Sporting clays ranges will incorporate many different shooting scenarios, ranging from shooting in a field under the bright sun to shots being fired in a wooded area with low light. It is recommended that a shooter equips him/herself with shooting glass that have several different lens tints to accommodate various lighting conditions. Some lens colors may also make the orange of the clay target stand out more. As with any outdoor activity, bugs will be in abundance. Using insect repellent may help but be aware it can affect the wood finish on a gun.

Sporting clays has become very popular, as it is a very social game that allows for conversation to take place while moving on to the next station. Sporting clays has been referred to as golf with guns.

One can go to the same sporting clays range for years and never get bored, as many ranges will change up the scenarios frequently to keep their regular clients coming back. For example, one can have a left crosser shot paired up with an incoming target on station 5 which is in the woods. The next month that same station can have a teal machine (which launches clays straight up in the air) and an outgoing crosser. Even different times of year will change the look of the terrain, thus changing the target presentation. As you see, the possibilities are endless.

5-Stand

5-stand is a game that is a combination of hunting scenarios similar to sporting clays but a condensed version. Where in sporting clays you need several acres to make a good course, you need far less with 5-stand. At some ranges the 5-Stand is no larger than a skeet field. It is the perfect game when you don't have enough time to shoot a round of sporting clays and it is by far cheaper as you only shoot twenty-five shots per round verses the one hundred in sporting clays. Some of the presentations you will see in 5-stand are a clay target rolling and bouncing on its edge (simulates a running jumping rabbit), or a slow incomer that represents a bird coming in for landing. As in Sporting Clays, ranges move the target machines around to change the course so it is always challenging for the returning shooter.

Rifle and Pistol Competitions

The NRA is the governing body for Rifle and Pistol programs and competitions. You will find Rifle and Pistol competitions across the nation at the local level that are for competitors ranging from first timers with no classification to advanced competitors shooting shoulder to shoulder in sanctioned matches. Once you have competed in your first local competition, you may want to consider continuing by shooting in regional, state, and national sanctioned matches. To find match dates, you can visit NRA's Competitive Shooting Division for their online calendar at www.competitions.nra.org.

As with shotgun, rifle and pistol events have their place in the Olympics. Each of the disciplines have several different events and US athletes have brought home their share of medals. USA Shooting is the governing body for Olympic shooting which covers air rifle, air pistol and .22 rifle and pistol.

New on the horizon is the NRA America's Rifle Challenge (ARC). It is a recreational training event designed to develop modern shooting skills with general purpose rifles, such as the AR-15 or any other semi-automatic rifle with a detachable magazine. ARC events are designed for shooters of all skill levels and can be conducted on almost any center-fire range in the country. Attendees will learn safe firearm handling skills with their personal firearms and gear while having fun in an athletic shooting environment.

NRA America's Rifle Challenge (ARC)

Cowboy-action particpants, photo courtesy of Single Action Shooting Society

Cowboy-Action Shooting

Cowboy-action shooting originated in Southern California in the early 1980s and is now practiced throughout the US. While there are several sanctioning organizations, the most well known is the Single Action Shooting Society (SASS). Cowboy-action is a type of three-gun match utilizing a combination of time period revolvers, rifles, and shotguns in a variety of Old West–themed courses of fire, where both time and accuracy count for score. Participants must dress in appropriate theme or era costume and use the gear required by the sanctioning group. A unique and clever element of cowboy-action shooting is the adoption of an alias, such as "Marshal Halloway" or "Pantaloon Pam," for which the participant develops his or her own costume. "It is a liberating part of the experience of stepping back in history and playing cowboys and Indians for real," according to the SASS website.

Cowboy-action requires competitors to use firearms typical of the mid-to-late nineteenth century when the saga of the cowboy first scored in the American imagination: single-action revolvers, lever-action rifles chambered in pistol calibers, and side-by-side double-barrel shotguns (called coach guns) or pump-action shotguns with external hammers. Both original and reproduction guns are equally acceptable. Cowboy competition generally requires four guns: two revolvers, a shotgun, and a rifle chambered in a centerfire revolver caliber of a type used prior to 1899. Some CAS matches also offer side events for single-shot "buffalo rifles" or derringers, and others have limitations on ammunition by "power factor" (calculated by multiplying the bullet weight in grains and the muzzle velocity in feet per second and then dividing the result by one thousand), or by muzzle velocity (often 1,000 fps for pistols and 1,400 fps for rifles).

A unique opportunity in cowboy shooting is the opportunity to compete on horseback. Participants ride their own horses and shoot their way through a patterned course of fire, which gives the image of a cowboy-action mounted shooter. Riders race through a series of obstacles while using two .45-caliber single-action revolvers, loaded with five rounds each of black-powder blanks to shoot ten balloon targets set in a special random pattern or Old West–type scenario.

Typically, a competitor crosses the timing beam at a full gallop and engages the first pattern of five targets. After a shooter fires the fifth shot, he or she returns the empty revolver to a holster and proceeds to the next set of five targets. The contestant with the fastest accumulated time wins.

Because of the exciting nature of cowboy-action shooting and the enthusiasm of participants, safety is a special consideration at every venue. Safety or ballistic glasses must be worn at all times. In a typical stage or shooting setup the shooter who is next in line to compete will load his guns at a loading table under the supervision of a designated loading official. Western-style "six-shooters" are always loaded with only five rounds with the empty chamber under the hammer. The shooter's rifle will also be loaded with the requisite number of rounds with the hammer down on an empty chamber. Shotguns are always left unloaded, then loaded "on the clock."

At a typical cowboy-action range, guns are kept unloaded except when the shooter prepares at the loading table and is shooting the stage. He or she then proceeds to the unloading table to unload the revolvers and demonstrate that all guns are empty. Even with empty guns, cowboy-action range officials emphasize safe shooting—a fun experience that can last a lifetime.

A range officer is responsible for safely conducting the shooter through the stage. The range officer's attention is not on the targets but rather on the shooter and his firearms. One important duty of the range officer is to immediately stop the shooter if the shooter's gun or ammunition is defective in any unsafe way.

Camp Perry Smallbore

3-Gun Competition

3-Gun shooting is one of the fastest-growing shooting sports in the world. It is featured as fast-moving and requires competitors to become proficient with three different firearms: the modern sporting rifle, a semi-automatic pistol, and a shotgun. A 3-Gun match is not a stationary event and it seeks to test one's physical and tactical abilities. Participants must move through different stages and engage targets in a variety of different positions. Each stage generally requires the use of different firearms and requires that the shooter smoothly and rapidly transition between them.

Shooters will shoot at a variety of targets, such as clay targets, steel targets, or cardboard silhouettes. But because the sport has not yet become over-organized, match organizers still have a great deal of leeway to produce a safe and enjoyable shooting venue. Target distances can range from one to five hundred yards and the winning participant will have to score the most hits in the least amount of time, although some targets are designated "friendlies" and shooting them will reduce a participant's score.

Competitors mainly shoot modern sporting rifles in .223 calibre with short, 18- to 20-inch barrels and 30-round magazines. Any semi-auto that handles larger magazines is usually permitted but has to be in compliance with state and local laws. Any safe, reliable semi-auto or pump-action shotgun is used and should include an extended magazine tube and interchangeable chokes. In most 3-Gun competitions, shot shells and slugs are used. For pistols, most shooters prefer 9mm semi-automatics, but other calibers can be used depending on what division the match is being conducted. Accessories are simple and usually limited to a holster for the pistol and a belt pouch for extra ammo magazines.

Recently the NRA Recreational Programs and Ranges Division has developed the NRA 3-Gun Experience program which is a fun, exhilarating, and physical activity to expose new and intermediate shooters to the wonderful world of 3-Gun. To broaden exposure to shooting, the NRA 3-Gun Experience program is a safe, family-fun, and mildly competitive, recreational event. Utilizing modern sporting .22 rifles, .22 pistols, and shotguns, as well as airsoft rifles, pistols, and shotguns, this activity is designed to fully equip participants with the same firearms and ammunition to give them a level playing field.

The NRA 3-Gun Experience Guidebook is available for digital download at www. nrasports.nra.org and "is intended to provide a starting point to help clubs and ranges develop their own 3-Gun Experience Event, all while reaching new shooters and encouraging existing members to continue to show their support with this new and exciting activity."

Black-powder competition

Camp Perry pistol match

Treating firearms with care and respect does not at all diminish their enjoyment. The thrill of hitting a small dot in the center of the target at long range; the prospect of falling a deer due to a clean shot; the joy in shattering a clay target to dust; these are all part of the safe-shooting equation.

"Shooting in the open" means hunting or recreational plinking. Both require that the shooter be ultra-conscious of his or her responsibilities. Certainly, the primary imperatives apply:

• <u>ALWAYS</u> keep the gun pointed in a safe direction.
• <u>ALWAYS</u> keep your finger off the trigger until ready to shoot.
• <u>ALWAYS</u> keep the gun unloaded until ready to use.
• Know your target and what is beyond.
• Know how to use the gun safely.
• Be sure the gun is safe to operate.
• Use only the correct ammunition for the gun.
• Wear eye and ear protection as appropriate.
• Never use alcohol or drugs before or while shooting.
• Store guns so they are not accessible to unauthorized persons.
• Be aware that certain types of guns and many shooting activities require additional safety precautions.

Hunter Orange

Safe shooting begins with pulling on your coat and boots before picking up your rifle, before entering the woods or calling the dog to hop into the back of the pickup. It begins by knowing what your state's requirements are for special clothing. Of course, you have to dress for the weather—layering with woolens or synthetics when it is cold and light cottons when it is warm—but almost every state requires a color of exterior garb known as "hunter orange" or "blaze orange."

Even in New York State, for instance, where hunter orange is not required by law, more than 80 percent of big-game hunters, as well as two out of three small-game hunters, wear some hunter orange. It just makes sense, because the structure of their eyes does not allow deer and other game animals to recognize the color in the same way as humans.

Deer and humans have different sensitivity to various wavelengths of light. Deer see short-wavelength colors such as blue (and even ultra-violet, which humans cannot detect with the naked eye) brighter than humans. Lacking red-sensitive cone cells in their eyes, deer are less sensitive to longer wavelengths such as orange and red, so these colors look darker to deer; that means they cannot distinguish red or orange from green and brown.

Wearing hunter orange saves lives because the brilliant orange color helps prevent other hunters from mistaking a person for an animal. According to

New York State statistics, hunters who wear hunter orange are seven times less likely to be mistaken for an animal. For example, during the past ten years, not one person who was wearing hunter orange was mistaken for game and shot in New York.

Browning Safety Blaze Vest

It is important to remember that when you go hunting you will not be the only hunter out there. You want to make sure you're visible and identifiable as a human being.

State regulations often mandate a minimum requirement (or none at all) for the wearing of hunter orange. Here are a couple of generalized examples:

• In Missouri, you must wear hunter orange during firearms deer season, a hat and shirt, vest or coat, and the color must be plainly visible from all sides. Camouflage orange does not satisfy this rule. (Missouri makes a few exceptions, such as hunting migratory game birds and archery.)

• In Pennsylvania, the "fluorescent orange" requirements are much more specific. During all small-game, deer, bear, and elk seasons, for instance, the state requires a "minimum of 250 square inches on head, chest, and back combined, visible 360 degrees." The Keystone State is very detailed in its approach to where, when, and how much orange must be worn.

• In Wyoming, all big-game hunters must wear one or more exterior garments (a hat, shirt, jacket, coat, vest, or sweater) of hunter orange. (The exception is bowhunters during a special archery season.)

Because state regulations are reviewed each year and often change, you must check for licensing regulations updates each time you purchase a hunting license. Wearing blaze orange is a large part of your safety equation.

Carrying Your Gun

Big game such as deer and feral hogs can be taken with rifles, muzzleloaders, and even handguns. If you are hunting with a revolver or pistol, usually a long-barrel single-shot firearm, with any scope affixed to the gun, this will prevent conventional holstering. But you can err on the safe side by entering and leaving the woods with the gun unloaded and the handgun in a case or daypack.

Long guns—rifles and shotguns—are more complex if only because there are millions more long-gun hunters than handgun hunters. A variety of carry options depend on the type of gun and the venue.

In the two-hand or ready position the firearm is carried with the muzzle end up and across the body. This is one of the safest carry positions because you have both hands firmly on the gun. It offers good muzzle control while allowing you to get into a shooting position quickly. This carry is often seen when hunters are

stalking a game animal or "still-hunting" (warily and slowly walking an area in search of a game animal) and is safe when others are in front of or behind you. It is not a safe approach when someone is on the same side that the muzzle is pointed.

With the cradle carry, one hand is on or near the grip while the fore-end of the firearm is cradled in your elbow. This is a comfortable way to carry a firearm, but this position is not as secure as a two-hand carry. You see hunters carrying guns in this position when they are crossing long patches of ground or perhaps climbing a hill

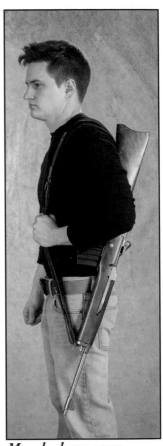

Muzzle-up carry

Muzzle-down carry

so they can observe the lower terrain. Use it when others are behind or in front of you, but never to the side where the muzzle is pointing.

Using the elbow or side carry requires that the firearm be tucked under your armpit and over the arm in front of the elbow. It's a safe method when walking in open terrain, but in brushy country, branches tend to catch the gun. Use it when others are behind or to your side, but not when they are in front of you.

Hunters (and other shooters, too) often use the trail carry by gripping their firearm firmly with one hand at the balance point. This carry offers very poor control of a gun if you were to trip or fall. Use it when hunting alone or when others are behind you or to your side. Never use this carry when someone is walking ahead of you.

A sling carry allows you to hang your firearm from your shoulder by a sling with the muzzle pointing upward. When you are standing, this carry method frees up your hands for things such as climbing or scanning terrain with binoculars. It's tough to keep a sling on your shoulder when walking, and some grasp the sling with one hand to keep the firearm from slipping off. Unless you have pulled the sling over your head so that the rifle or shotgun rests on your back at an angle, this is a relatively poor carry method when walking on difficult terrain or in heavy brush.

When one hand grasps the firearm at the grip while the firearm rests across the top of the shoulder, think of the carry

Cross-body carry

position as a shoulder carry. People who are tired after a day in the field will often resort to this position, as a rifle with a long barrel and wood stock may weigh eight to nine pounds. This is however the least safe of all carries, as you have little control over the firearm should you fall. Never use it when someone is behind you or while walking on rough terrain.

Above all, never carry or pass a gun with your finger on the trigger or the safety off. The mechanical safety is not a guarantee that the cartridge cannot fire. Such a technique provides an additional measure of insurance and, with your finger off the trigger, you have almost a 100 percent chance of moving safely.

Treestands: Opportunity and Danger

Hunting deer from trees first became popular with archery hunters who needed to be extremely close to make a good shot. Today, many firearm hunters have also taken to the heights. From a safety perspective, hunting from trees offers enormous advantages along with some disadvantages.

The three great advantages of today's lightweight, portable treestands relate to view, scent, and concealment. Because a stand may be positioned twenty or more feet above the ground, it allows a superior view of your surroundings. This is not only great for identifying game, but it is a safety consideration as well. A hunter on a high stand can quickly see game and what is behind or around it. Unless it hits some deflecting branch (or you miss), you will be able to see where your bullet travels. Hunting "on high" helps eliminate "sound shots" or the I-thought-it-was-a-deer syndrome.

The second benefit of a treestand, though unrelated directly to safety, is that your human scent is raised off the ground. Deer and elk are particularly sensitive to odors, and hunting from elevated platforms will elevate your scent and more readily move it downwind away from their noses.

The third benefit of a treestand is concealment. While any movement may give away your presence, good discipline on stand—sitting still and quietly, refusing to scratch or answer your cell phone—generally gives you the best and most consistent opportunity to harvest a game animal, although great advances have been made recently in the development of ground blinds. Typically, deer do not look up, so a treestand will elevate you above their line of sight.

Hunting from treestands also presents disadvantages. You have very little mobility, and moving for a better view or making a shot can be impaired by the trees around and brush below. From a distance, deer can see you without looking up. You are conspicuous in a tree when you drink coffee from the thermos on a cold day or stretch your cramped legs. And although they may come with carry straps, even the best treestands are heavy and awkward to use. Strapping one to your back and carrying it into the woods along with your rifle, ammo, first-aid kit, knife, water, and everything else the modern hunter relies on for a successful outing can be daunting.

The greatest single consideration when deciding to hunt from a treestand, however—all advantages and disadvantages aside—is that they can be dangerous. Use of a treestand requires you to climb a tree, an increasingly difficult task as we get older and heavier; you then stand on a small surface. Getting on and off a treestand safely is often the most challenging moment. Unfortunately, serious injuries and deaths from treestand falls are common. Once on the stand, you must know where you are in relation to the edge of the platform. Even if you spot game, you can't focus on the target to the detriment of your own spatial awareness. There's also a risk of nodding off to sleep while waiting for game to show up.

It is also a good idea to use fall restraints and harnesses when in a treestand. Fall restraints tether a hunter to the tree, not the manufactured metal treestand. There are many styles of restraints and harnesses available and even some that will lower you to the ground slowly in case of a fall.

ACL505-A Magnum Climbing Treestand from API Outdoors

A fall restraint is not only for the time you're occupying the stand with your rifle across your lap. It's important to wear the restraints from the moment you begin your climb until the moment you're safely back on the ground again. If your restraint does not have a slow-release system that can lower you to the ground, you must have a plan to safely lower yourself, climb back into the stand, or reach your treesteps when your restraint system catches you after a fall.

When hunting from a treestand, you need to practice firearms security from the moment you begin to climb. This means always climbing and descending with an unloaded gun. Many hardcore but safety-conscious hunters tie a line from a limb or even the stand itself for lifting and lowering their gun. An excellent idea, but wait until you are on the stand and personally secure before pulling your rifle (or shotgun if you are shooting slugs) up after you. When you're ready to come down, lower your unloaded rifle to the ground first. Never climb up to or down from a treestand with a loaded gun.

Most big-game hunting hours end about a half-hour after sunset. The day is growing dim and this is the time to unload your gun, lower it to the ground, and adjust your fall-restraint harness so that you can also descend safely. Even though it may be tempting to wait because game is nearby, never climb or descend from a treestand in the dark. So much can happen to make this a hazardous moment, from snagging a wedding ring on the lip of a treestep to slipping because your boots are caked with mud or the steps are wet from rain.

Homemade treestands have been around for generations. The crumbling old platform in the deer woods is a symbol not only of natural decay but of our hunting and gun-carrying freedoms. Nevertheless, homemade treestands can be dangerous. Never climb into anyone else's stand without permission and even then, unless you are the builder or owner, you cannot be sure of the sturdiness of the platform. Wooden boards nailed to a tree are not a good ladder. Nails can easily be pulled out, and the wooden steps and platform deteriorate.

The Treestand Manufacturer's Association (TMA), has sought to develop safety standards for both stands and all manner of climbing apparatus. It was formed at a time when safety was a primary issue with the commercial stand business. Today, the TMA devotes its resources to treestand safety through education in the proper use of treestands, the development of treestand and harness-test standards, manufacturing quality control, and the promotion of mandatory use of fall-arrest systems, specifically a full-body harness.

A TMA label or hang tag on a stand at your retail outlet is assurance that the stand is well built and the manufacturer will stand behind the product. Generally, if used in accordance with the published recommendations and limits, a TMA stand is recognized as a safe platform. The TMA requires its manufacturer members to actively seek certification of conformance to association standards on all treestand and harness products. TMA product testing and certification is accomplished by independent testing firms.

More Ideas for Safe Hunting "In the Open"

A simple, but often overlooked, recommendation is that you should hunt with at least one partner. Together, you and your partner can watch out for one another. If either of you has an accident, the other can assist the injured party or go for help. Without a partner, you're on your own. Something as simple as a twisted ankle can become a life-threatening situation under the right circumstances.

It's doubly important to work with a partner if you'll be hunting in unfamiliar terrain. Together, you stand a better chance at navigating through the area and having a positive hunting experience than you would on your own.

Hunting with a partner not only provides personal insurance in any emergency, but a partner will assist in any number of situations including moving downed game—which can be a big chore if you're alone—to building a blind. Hunt with a buddy. It's safe and it's smart.

If you choose to hunt alone—and many thousands do to maximize the peace of the fields and forests—you should tell other people your plans. Let a spouse or friend know when and where you'll be hunting. Establish a time when you'll touch base with that person to let him or her know you're fine. If you are injured, you don't want the added danger of being left alone in the woods without anyone knowing where you are.

People experienced in the outdoors always carry a few simple items that can save their lives. A flashlight will help you avoid stumbling upon entering or leaving the woods in the dark. If you hunt into the evening hours, a flashlight helps identify you as a human being, too. Should you become a casualty of a fall or branch across the eyes, a flashlight will immeasurably aid in signaling searchers.

Even if you are not injured, a device as simple as a whistle can save your life. A scream, measured at just twenty-four feet, can be as loud as 60 decibels. A cheap storm or safety whistle, on the other hand, creates a clear, high-frequency sound with a power rating more than 75 percent greater than that of referee and safety whistles. They will double the reach and volume of the human voice with an unmistakable screech. They can even be heard up to fifty feet under water.

The third item that should be in your pocket is a knife that can be used to cut the safety line if you fall. In "the old days," hunters felt not only that they were invulnerable but that a simple rope around the waist and tied to the tree— annoying as that was—would save them if they fell out of a treestand. Too many unfortunate circumstances have proven that neither of those ideas was correct. Even a fall-arrest safety harness can fail. You must have some way of reaching the tree or releasing the harness, and with your weight holding the harness strap

Be sure to practice those shooting positions you may need to use in the open.

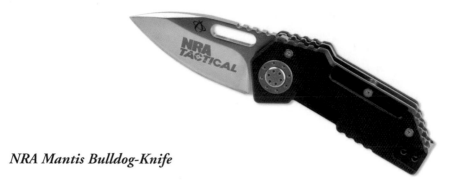

NRA Mantis Bulldog-Knife

tightly around your waist and chest, just breathing may soon become difficult. In the event that your harness does not allow you to reach the ground, that knife in your pocket can save your life once you cut the harness free. A fall onto your feet from a dozen feet (rather than onto your head and neck from twenty feet after falling asleep without wearing the harness) just could be the "least worst" scenario.

A knife has its own danger, though, through careless use around camp or in field dressing game. One slip with a sharp knife blade can slice open an artery. (With a severe cut, you may have only a minute to staunch the blood before you pass out.) Field dressing and cutting up a big-game animal to haul out of the woods is a chore, a dangerous chore if you are the least bit inattentive with the knife.

Of course, the item that we rarely overlook when talking about hunting and shooting is the ubiquitous cell phone. Some purists and old-timers will not be caught dead in the forest with a smartphone, but a cell phone could save your life after an accident. The difficulty of course will be finding reception in the hunting fields and deep woods, but can be something to test when you're scouting for a place to hunt.

And speaking of cell phones …. Nothing is worse than hearing a phone go off during a concert, or at a tense moment in a movie, or in the deep silence of the woods. Silence your phone when you enter the woods and button it into a shirt pocket so that it can be available if you need it. But hunting is supposed to be an activity that takes you away from the everyday routine—and that means away from voice mail and the almost insatiable impulse to answer or silence a ringing phone. If you own and enjoy a smartphone, do take it to the treestand, but silence it for the duration, at least until you are back at the vehicle at the end of day.

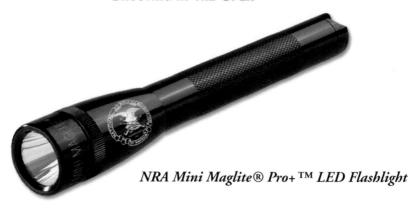

NRA Mini Maglite® Pro+™ LED Flashlight

Fitness for Hunters

This book is not trying to sell gym memberships, but it might as well be noted that some hunters are becoming older and less fit. These circumstances in themselves may become safety issues if older hunters attempt to run and climb and hunt in as carefree a manner as they did a generation ago. This is not to suggest that you should become a couch potato. Far from it! To live healthier and longer, an active lifestyle is always preferable to one that is inactive, and hunting offers dramatic and positive benefits.

Unfortunately, every hunting season is marred by a rash of heart attacks. Heart attacks take a higher toll than any careless hunting practice, even than treestand accidents, given the increasing use of full-body fall-arrest harnesses. Hiking while carrying ten or twenty pounds of gear, the excitement of spotting and shooting at a big-game animal, and then field dressing and dragging a carcass can cause more stress than the sedentary heart can handle. That's especially true if you smoke, drink excessively, or have high blood pressure, elevated cholesterol, or other health problems. (Consider carrying aspirin in your daypack and should you have any doubt about its efficacy or whether it is appropriate, check first with your doctor.)

If you don't exercise regularly, the unaccustomed excitement and exertion in the field can be dangerous. Begin building endurance before hunting season, especially if you're planning a "dream hunt" to the mountains for elk or to Alaska for Dahl Sheep—places where you have to walk every day and carry your guns and gear. You don't have to train as if you are going to run a marathon. Any activity that forces you to move, from tennis to dancing to raking leaves, will help strengthen your heart and lungs.

Walking is a simple, easy way to strengthen your heart and lungs, tone muscles, and generally improve fitness. Little is required beyond comfortable shoes and the willingness to improve your health. Brisk walking burns up to 440 calories an hour. Walking three mph burns 250 to 315 calories per hour. You can lose a pound of fat by burning 3,500 calories. Decide what your body can do comfortably. If you have been inactive, proceed slowly and build up.

CLEANING YOUR FIREARMS

Shooting a clean firearm is step one in safe shooting and gun handling.

Mom taught us that cleanliness is next to godliness. That same mom hustled us outdoors after school: "Go outside, play, but don't get dirty." Even if she did not recognize the contradiction, she connected us with the world outside of television or our stereos. Guns, like children left to have fun and enjoy the outdoors, naturally get dirty.

Pulling the trigger of any firearm means the gun gets dirty. Residue from the powder burn or even the bullet itself builds up in the barrel. Soot (from the powder and the primer) and copper fouling (from the bullet jacket) are deposited in the gun. At some point, these materials will interfere with its action and cause a malfunction.

Guns do not have to be spotless if you're planning to shoot sporting clays, take part in 3-Gun competitions, go hunting, or try a little cowboy-action games. It only has to be functional and reliable, but a well-maintained firearm speaks volumes to other participants. It tells them you're an individual who is careful and pays attention. It suggests that you are a person they can trust to stand alongside on the firing line.

Gun care is not a "sexy" topic. Cleaning a dirty gun can be messy and leave oil stains on your clothes and rags. For some, cleaning is a lackadaisical activity. That should never be the case. Cleaning your gun deserves the same amount of concentration and respect as firing it.

The primary rule of handling any firearm is to know, without a doubt, if it is loaded. Whether you are field-stripping a gun for maintenance or showing it off to a friend, the gun must be unloaded. No excuses.

Verifying there is no cartridge in the chamber is easier with some guns than others. An empty revolver is easy to mechanically eyeball; less so a semi-automatic pistol or rifle. The first step is always to make sure the gun is unloaded, even before finding a good place to start cleaning.

Where you work is important. Chemicals are noxious and can be toxic if ingested. If you choose the kitchen table, spread a large plastic trash bag over it with newspaper pages on top. Optionally, use a Gun Cleaning Mat: non-skid bottom, absorbent top, and machine washable. Run a fan or the air conditioner for ventilation because if your spouse is nearby cooking dinner, the fumes will not enhance anyone's appetite.

Old-timers may scoff, but it's reasonable to wear safety glasses, and even protective gloves, in order to reduce exposure to toxic materials. Once you are finished cleaning (or shooting), wash your hands and the tabletop in hot, soapy water. Use the same rule as for camping and leave the area cleaner than how you found it.

122

Make sure your firearm is unloaded before cleaning.

Use bore cleaning solvent to moisten and lubricate the brush before cleaning the barrel.

The first place you disassemble, clean, and reassemble your gun should be at home. It will inevitably be a learning experience.

The Professionals Speak

Otis Technology manufactures gun-care kits and develops educational literature for gun owners. Its six fundamentals for cleaning a gun are a good place to begin.

1. Clean breech-to-muzzle in the direction of the bullet's travel.
Fire a gun, and extreme temperatures and pressures push the bullet (or the pellets) forward. Residues are left behind. Pushing a brush or patch from the muzzle toward the chamber shoves this residue and accumulated moisture into the less-polluted chamber and receiver elements. This can cause cartridge cases to stick, and problems with lever-action and auto-loading firearms.

From the breech end, push the brush all the way through the bore, then pull it back through.

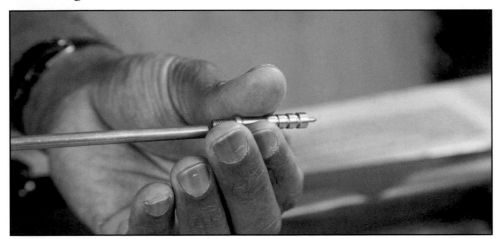

Remove the brush and use a jag to push a cleaning patch through the barrel.

Patches get dirty. Use a clean patch surface each time you swab the barrel.

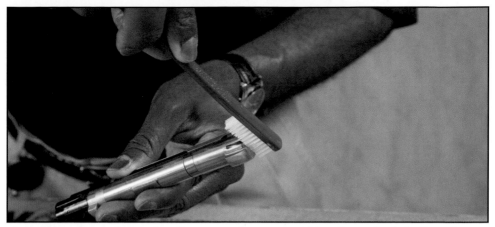

A toothbrush can be used to loosen and remove residue from the bolt, breech, and many other parts.

You can do a partial cleaning of hard-to-reach areas by flushing with a solvent that leaves no residue.

2. Center the tip of the cleaning rod. Don't let it scrape against the bore.
Firearms record their history in the barrel: age, number of shots taken, and overall level of maintenance. This is why gun purchasers will inspect the bore. A barrel's steel is harder than the materials of a bullet or shot pellets, and certainly harder than lightweight aluminum or carbon cleaning rods. Still, scratches can result when the tip or the rod itself carelessly scrapes the inside of the barrel.

3. Use a clean patch surface each time you swab the barrel.
Think of mopping the floor but never rinsing the mop. Every firearm accumulates abrasive grime in the bore and action. A patch with solvent applied will soak this slop and pull it out, but used repeatedly, a dirty patch only redeposits crud back in the gun. Subsequent rounds fired pick up this dirt and slowly erode the throat. It's the equivalent of cleaning in the wrong direction. Patches are cheap; change them often. A generous spraying with a product like Hoppe's Elite Gun Cleaner gives even faster results, though it must then be followed by swabbing with clean patches.

Use a solvent-moistened soft cloth to clean the outer surfaces.

Rifle lubrication points include the body of the bolt.

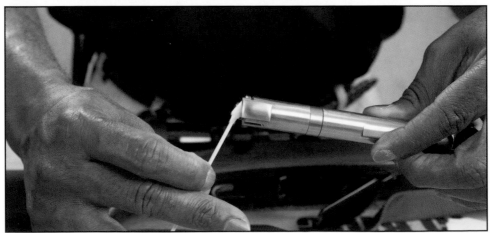

 The bolt face and firing pin mechanism.

4. Never run a dry brush down a barrel.
A wire brush plus a dry barrel equal bore damage, or a brush with broken bristles. Effective bore and brush cleaning requires use of a lubricating solvent. Still, cleaning experts disagree about dipping or spraying a brush in solvent before sliding it through the barrel; the brush spindle collects dirt and thus must be sprayed with a solvent such as Break-Free's Power Blast. Power Blast is a citrus-based, environmentally friendly product for use at the range or in the field.

5. Never scrub back and forth, reversing the brush inside the bore.
This practice, perhaps left over from teenage chores, quickly ruins a brush by bending the bristles. Imagine bending a wire back and forth until it breaks. Brush in a consistent direction, pushing or pulling breech-to-muzzle, to preserve the effectiveness of the brush.

6. Use only a few drops of solvent or lubricant.
If a little bit is good, is more better? Not for gun care. Too much solvent can damage a firearm, stain and weaken the wood of the grip, stock, and forearm, drip into the trigger housing, and become difficult to completely remove. Solvent or oil in the receiver can cause a gummy trigger. It just isn't necessary to use more than a couple of drops of solvent per patch.

If the barrel is removable, consider giving it a soaking shot of cleaner-degreaser spray such as Tetra Gun's Action Blaster before using a brush or patch.

Meet Your Tools

Numerous reputable companies offer gun-cleaning kits and supplies. You can certainly put a kit together "from scratch" but as a newcomer to gun care, it might not be a bad idea to begin with a kit.

Kits are inexpensive and contain all or most of the required pieces. After cleaning your firearm a few times, it will be time to refresh the supplies—an excellent time to experiment with components that may work better for your particular gun.

A kit typically includes one or more cleaning rods, bore brushes, a patch loop, cleaning patches, solvent, and lubricant. It may also contain items designed to protect you from chemicals while you work: rubber gloves and protective goggles.

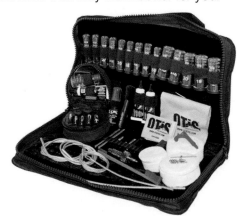

The parts of a kit come together as a cleaning system:

Otis Extreme cleaning kit

Lubricate the inside of the receiver and other areas where parts contact each other under pressure.

For level-actions, lubricate the hammer components.

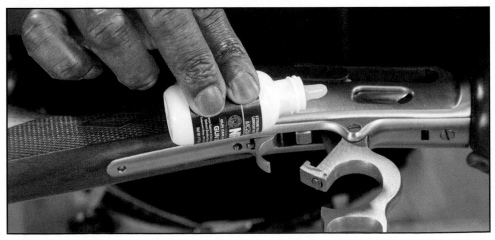

 The lever mechanism and slide component should be oiled as well.

1. The bore rod usually comes in several segments that screw together. A scrub brush, jag, or patch loop screws onto one end, the handle at the other. The rod must be long enough to reach from the bore into the chamber. An attachment such as a brush can be screwed onto the end and drawn breech-to-muzzle to pull debris out of the gun. Most cleaning requires several passes of

NRA cleaning kit

the brush. After a few initial runs, unscrew the brush and spray it with solvent to remove adhering grime. Cleaning rods come in several sizes and it is important to purchase the correct length and diameter for your gun. A multi-segment rod for a 12-gauge shotgun with a 28-inch barrel probably won't work for a short-barrelled rifle, much less a pistol. Fortunately, cleaning gear is cheap and should be purchased when purchasing the gun.

2. The scrub brush is bore-specific. Use a brush sized to the caliber, a .38 brush in a .38 (or .357), for example. Forcing a .45 brush through the bore of that .38 might ruin the brush, damage the bore's interior finish, and ruin your gun's accuracy. A brush is usually stamped with bore size. Brushes come in several materials, including nylon and copper, but are most commonly brass. A brass wire brush is probably the best all-around brush for pushing build-up out of a barrel. Stainless steel brushes should not be used in the bore.

3. The screw-in eyelet or loop for a cleaning patch is often made of plastic, a suitable material for this task. While the threads are easy to strip, a new loop costs pennies and it can never scratch the interior of a firearm. Just pull the patch through the loop as if you were threading a needle and drip on solvent. A better option than the traditional loop is a screw-in jag, either brass or plastic. A jag pushes a patch through the barrel. While the patch in a loop may or may not maintain constant pressure against the bore, a jag, machined slightly smaller than the bore and ridged to hold the patch tightly, solves this problem. Simply drape a patch over the jag's point and insert it in the bore. Because this combination is almost exactly the size of the bore, it makes better contact with lands and grooves. A fitted jag reduces the number of trips a patch must take down the bore and helps extend the life of your firearm.

4. Neither a jag nor a loop works without a cleaning patch attached. Cotton or synthetic, patches come in several sizes. Cotton easily absorbs solvent or lubricant and is the traditional material for swabbing out grime. Microfiber or polyester does not leave threads of lint behind, particles that can absorb humidity and become a spot source of rust.

Whichever type of patch you choose—truly budget-conscious shooters make patches from old tee shirts and dryer sheets—purchase them by the hundreds. Patches are cheap but essential. Discard immediately when they become dirty.

5. Solvents help remove fouling. Use solvents on brushes and on patches. As you learn gun cleaning, use a general-purpose solvent such as Hoppe's No. 9. Avoid copper solvents at first because they are extremely harsh and can ruin brushes. As your shooting becomes more specialized, your interest in accuracy will become more intense. That's the time to experiment with specialized cleaners to attack carbon or copper buildup.

Particular solvents may be required for different ammunition types. The firearms-cleaning industry was built on the lead-bullet premise, but today's options include copper and brass bullets, synthetic bullet tips, steel and tungsten shot, and a complexity of powders and components. Thus solvents have become specialized in application, which means cleaning equipment itself may be susceptible to chemical reactions and must also be cleaned.

A solvent can even be sprayed directly down a barrel, breech-to-muzzle, to help loosen the grime in the barrel grooves that a patch can sometimes skip over in the tough spots. While some shooters believe solvent in the action is not a bad thing—it eventually evaporates and the bolt face and other parts must also be cleaned—we nevertheless hold with Otis that effective cleaning is directed out the muzzle.

6. The final step is lubricant; the key is "use sparingly." Use a very light application, perhaps on a Q-tip, between metal-to-metal parts or on shiny wear-spots. Otherwise, your gun will smell like a refinery and the excess oil will attract dust and grit. Then, as performance deteriorates, you will blame the lubricant when the actual cause will simply be using too much.

In "the old days," when Dad showed us his World War II souvenirs or the Colt .45 he brought home, they used heavy oil, even grease, on weapons. Some of these older guns were even dipped in a coating chemical preservative called "cosmoline." No longer. Find an old gun—perhaps a gun in the C&R, curio, and relic, category (generally guns more than fifty years old)—at an auction that is greased up or has been dipped in cosmoline and you will need to spend several hours cleaning before you fire it: scrub all parts, wood and metal, with mineral spirits.

7. Sold by Hornady, Brownells, and others, ultrasonic cleaning systems are electrically powered cleaning tanks that use a combination of ultrasound, heat, and cleaning solvent to scrub small objects quickly. These setups save time and produce good results for gun club members or a shooter with several guns or who reloads ammo.

Ultrasonic systems create scrubbing bubbles that remove powder fouling, lead and jacketed bullet fouling, light rust, and grease. Heat eliminates the need to use ammoniated cleaning solutions to get rid of copper fouling. With most firearms, only a basic field strip is required. Drop the parts into the machine's basket and the tank's cavitating action cleans everything microscopically in ten minutes.

Cleaning the Revolver

First, make sure the gun is unloaded. Swing out the cylinder and visually check the chambers. You might have a rare break-top revolver whose frame is hinged at the bottom front of the cylinder such as an old British Webley, but the principle is the same.

Verify that the gun is empty, then follow NRA's safety rules. If you need to unload the gun first, take the cartridges elsewhere. This keeps them away from the chemicals and from rolling off the table and under the sofa.

For single-action revolvers, the cylinder is removed from the frame. For double-action revolvers, simply swing the cylinder out into the open position. Look for buildup around the forcing cone, the face of the cylinder, and the cylinder ratchet. For double-action revolvers, check under the ejector star as well.

You might try tying a rag around the rear cylinder opening to protect from any damage when the brush is pushed through the barrel and to soak up any dripping solvent. Drip or spray solvent onto your brush before pushing it through the barrel, allowing it to twist to follow the rifling. Follow with cleaning patches generously sprinkled with more solvent. (There's no need to dip the absorbent patch in solvent. This causes a mess inside the gun and out.) Use as many patches as necessary and then follow with dry patches until a patch comes out clean. Clean each cylinder in the same manner.

Using an old toothbrush and solvent, scrub around the muzzle, the rear cylinder opening, and the front and rear of the cylinder itself. Brush and wipe the extractor rod and then push it out to clean the star and the rest of the rod normally housed between the cylinders. Leave no residue behind.

Last, with a small amount of gun oil, wipe the metal parts, inside the barrel, and the cylinders. Wipe off excess oil; then wipe the gun with a silicone gun cloth, perhaps from KleenBore. If it looks like your gun is greasy or oily, you're not finished. Revolvers need only a little lubrication. Single-actions need some lubrication on the cylinder pin and ratchet; double-actions need some on the ejector rod and cylinder ratchet.

There's no excuse to let a revolver deteriorate. Cleaning takes five minutes, ten if you are meticulous.

Cleaning the Pistol

Unlike a revolver, a pistol—a semi-automatic handgun—requires maintenance for continuous functioning. A pistol has several moving parts that ought to be cleaned and lubricated—not each time the trigger is pulled, but on a regular basis.

- First, verify the gun is unloaded and, even then, follow NRA's safety rules.
- Before shooting a new pistol, disassemble and reassemble it. Owner's manuals clarify the level of disassembly that can routinely be performed without voiding your warranty. The manual should also specify which points—generally between sliding metal parts—require lubrication, and guide you through handling the springs and levers inside.
- Your cleaning kit may be the same as that for a revolver, but consider adding a bore light or flashlight. Most semi-autos have black, non-reflective parts, and a bright light helps spot leftover grime in the interior. (Check Brownells for a variety of styles.)
- A pistol typically requires disassembly only into basic groups: barrel, slide, guide rod, frame, and magazine. Most of us will begin with the barrel, as it usually contains the most gunk. Begin cleaning with a bore brush, scrubbing with solvent; then patches, first coated with solvent; and ultimately, clean and dry until they come out of the bore unsoiled. Finally, apply a very light, thin layer of oil to protect the rifling.
- Clean additional components in the same manner. Just remember that a pistol has plenty of angles, nooks, and crannies, and generally requires more attention than a revolver. Be attentive to the slide's interior grooves, under the ejector, and the contact points between the slide and the frame. Here, such everyday artifacts as a toothbrush and Q-tips will be invaluable.
- Remember that a little solvent goes a long way. You may want to unscrew the grips and lay them aside to prevent contact with chemicals. Wipe clean of solvent before applying an ultra-light coating of lubricant such as Birchwood Casey's Moly Lube.
- Reassemble the pistol and cycle the action several times. This shocks the shooting system and evenly distributes the lubricant. It also assures you that everything still works correctly.
- The exterior also needs a light coating of gun oil, and wiping with a silicone cloth. Don't neglect the exterior because it must fend off the oil in your hands, dust, and lead particles at the shooting range.

Cleaning the Shotgun

Shotgun barrels collect an immense amount of fouling, including debris from the super-heated wads that carry the load of shot past the muzzle. Nevertheless, a light cleaning is fine for a pheasant hunt or trap shoot, saving thorough disassembly and cleaning for home.

Some shotguns are relatively complex tools but a bit vague on the mechanics. The single-shot or over/under is much simpler to clean than a pump-action or semi-automatic.

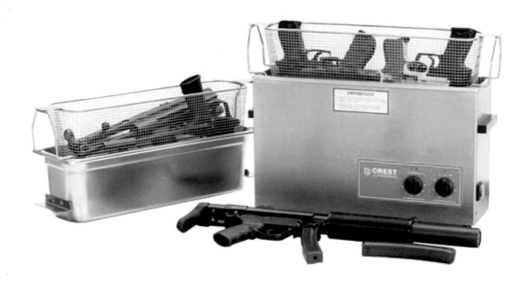

Crest Ultrasonic - F1200HT ultrasonic cleaning system

The before-and-after steps apply to shotguns as to handguns: Make sure the gun is unloaded, use as much solvent and gun oil as needed, but not a drop more, and work the action several times after reassembling the gun.

If you are traveling, it is vital to do a minimal cleaning at day's end. Remove the barrel and swab it. With solvent on a patch or rag, wipe the inside of the receiver. More depends on the use and the day. Get caught outside in the rain and you will also want to wipe the gun carefully with a silicone cloth.

With long guns in the field, it's important not to become overly enthusiastic. Small parts on a blanket inside a tent with a curious dog do not mix. The interior of semi-autos have a number of rods and springs that, incorrectly reassembled, may cause a failure. Avoid spraying solvents directly into a trigger unit, as the precision-machined and mounted parts are balanced and require smooth, lubricated operation. Concentrate on the barrel, gas chamber (if your gun has one), choke tubes, and spots showing metal-to-metal friction.

At the workbench, you can disassemble and clean any moving part of a semi-auto, any area where gas bleed-off might cause the buildup of crud.

Another name for a shotgun is a smoothbore. With no lands and grooves in the bore, the barrel is easier to clean, with one exception: the rifled barrel designed to fire slugs. These require scrubbing to remove fouling, but they will not have choke tubes, which require particular attention.

Field and sporting shotguns handle a variety of choke tubes that screw into the muzzle, and thus the threads of the choke and the bore need to be cleaned. (Always reinsert and tighten a choke after cleaning. Otherwise, in the excitement of shooting, it is easy to forget. Never fire a shotgun that is threaded for chokes without a choke tube in place. Doing so will ruin your shot and damage the choke threads.) Once you have scrubbed the threads, dry and apply a light coating of gun grease to prevent seizing.

In the field, you should clean and lube the action sparingly unless there is a special problem, but wipe down any pistons or spring assembly around semi-auto gas ports. Remember that lubricants attract dust, so remove obvious grime and finish with a visual inspection. Apply a superficial coat of oil to metallic surfaces, tighten screws and chokes, reassemble, and wipe down.

Cleaning the Rifle

A rifle is not essentially different when it comes to cleaning than a shotgun or pistol. Find a place to spread out and some way to hold the gun in place, such as a gun vise from MTM (excellent for any long gun) or sandbags or even a padded workbench vise (drape a towel over its jaws to prevent scratches).

Most rifles can be assembled with a screwdriver and a punch to push against the holding pins. Others, such as the M1 Garand, require specialized tools. While most gun owners believe they can field strip, clean, and reassemble their guns blindfolded, a take-down guide is a wonderful accessory, especially the first few times.

An often overlooked item is a hardware organizer from a company such as Plano Molding. Simply laying small parts on the cleaning pad is a good way to lose them among the tools or on the carpet. This can save hours of searching on hands and knees.

Rifle barrels are more difficult to clean than shotgun or pistol barrels. Rifles operate at much higher pressures, firing copper-jacketed bullets at high velocities. This causes the bullet's exterior to rub against and deposit scrapings on the rifling.

Remove the bolt assembly. Spray it with solvent and scrub the face and under the extractor with a toothbrush. Wipe or blow off the crud and chemical with a high-pressure hose or a can of compressed air. Allow the parts to dry before applying a light coating of gun oil.

Clean the barrel with the same actions and cautions as discussed with other guns, scrubbing with solvent and following with patches on a jag from chamber to muzzle. This direction ensures that you will not damage the crown on the muzzle. (A trued muzzle crown ensures that bullets exit the barrel

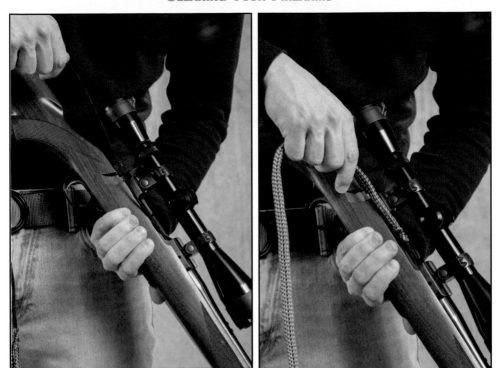

With a bore snake, you feed the thin line down the breech until you reach the thicker part.

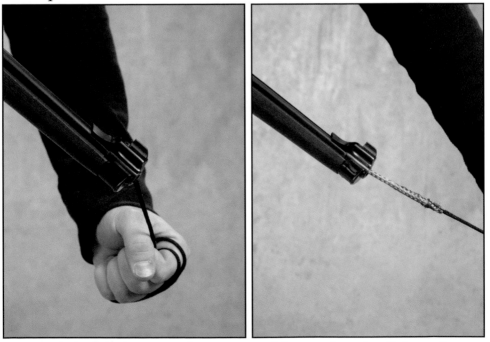

Next grab the line that is now hanging out of the muzzle and pull the snake through.

consistently on all surfaces, and thus fly straight.)

After scrubbing the bore six to eight times with brush and solvent, apply solvent and let the barrel stand for thirty minutes to soften any hard-to-remove grime. Then clean with patches as required. A green color on the patch indicates that the solution is dissolving copper debris. A couple of passes with a patch soaked in rust preventative and the bore is finished.

A C&R rifle (curio and relic, generally a collector's gun) has probably been fired a great deal and cleaned often. It will have a worn and wider bore by thousandths of an inch, but under rifle pressures this matters. Experimentation with several bore brush and jag diameters may be necessary.

Old guns such as the C&R variety, which may have been used in military conflicts or used with inferior powders, may have pitted barrels. You cannot return these to spotless condition, even with professional cleaning.

The modern sporting rifle (MSR) is extremely popular now and its disassembly is easy but requires following the service manual and perhaps a set of small Allen wrenches. The typical rifle has a plastic stock and so is not subject to chemical deterioration as is walnut, but solvents and plastics do not mix. Besides, lubricant on plastic leaves a slick spot that is difficult to remove. On the other hand, too little lubricant in an AR in hard use may cause a failure to cycle.

A Few Black-Powder Notes

Black powder and muzzleloading firearms have evolved since the Kentucky long rifle and, from a distance, may not look like black-powder guns at all. Yet because of the type of powders used, the guns require continuous cleaning because they are particularly susceptible to rust and corrosion. (Never substitute modern smokeless powder for black powder or Pyrodex unless the powder is specifically authorized for muzzleloaders.)

There are many black-powder designs— antique Brown Bess muskets from the Revolutionary War days to modern CVA Accura MRs—but effective cleaning for a rifle or handgun is hardly different than cleaning a modern firearm, although the amount of residue can be substantial. With black powder guns, soap and water should be used as opposed to cleaning solvents.

Disassemble the gun following the owner's manual. The only rule is not to tear apart something you can't fix. Remove the barrel, the breech plug if possible, and the primer-

Remove breech end cap.

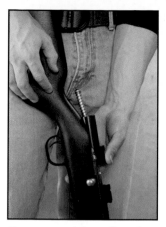

Remove guide rod and spring.

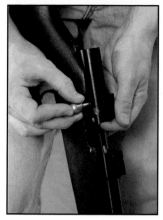

Remove bolt handle.

Push bolt out through breech.

Remove bolt.

Bolt extracted.

The nipple is now accessable.

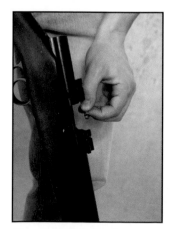

Remove the nipple.

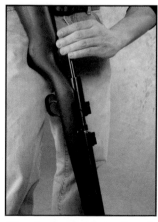

Use the appropriate tool to unthread nipple.

Remove breech plug.

nipple. If the gun is in ill repair, disassemble the stock from the trigger-housing assembly.

With the breech plug and/or nipple removed, the gun is easy to clean. Use a nipple pick or a needle to make sure there is no fouling in this tiny orifice. If it is fouled or plugged, you might experience poor ignition or a misfire. Soak a piece of thread in solvent, and run it back and forth through the orifice to prevent future fouling.from the Revolutionary War days to modern CVA Accura MRs— but effective cleaning for a rifle or handgun is hardly different than cleaning a modern firearm, although the amount of residue can be substantial.

Disassemble the gun following the owner's manual. The only rule is not to tear apart something you can't fix. Remove the barrel, the breech plug if possible, and the primer-nipple. If the gun is in ill repair, disassemble the stock from the trigger-housing assembly.

With the breech plug and/or nipple removed, the gun is easy to clean. Use a nipple pick or a needle to make sure there is no fouling in this tiny orifice. If it is fouled or plugged, you might experience poor ignition or a misfire. Soak a piece of thread in solvent, and run it back and forth through the orifice to prevent future fouling.

Submerge the muzzle in soapy water.

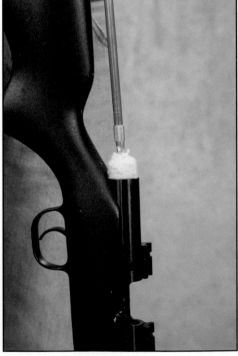

Push a 12-gauge cleaning swab through the bore.

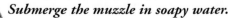

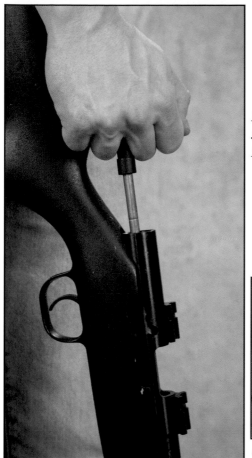

Pulling and pushing the swab will siphon soapy water into the barrel. Repeat until the barrel is clean.

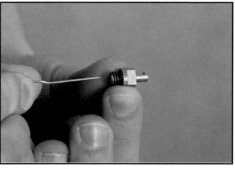

Cleaning the nipple with a paper clip

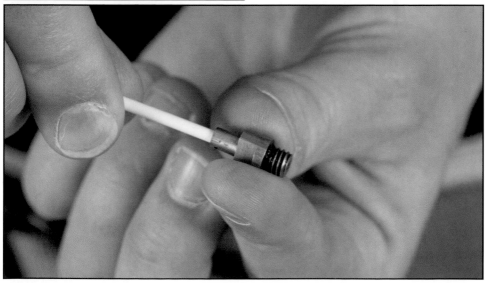

Using a pipe cleaner to finish cleaning the nipple

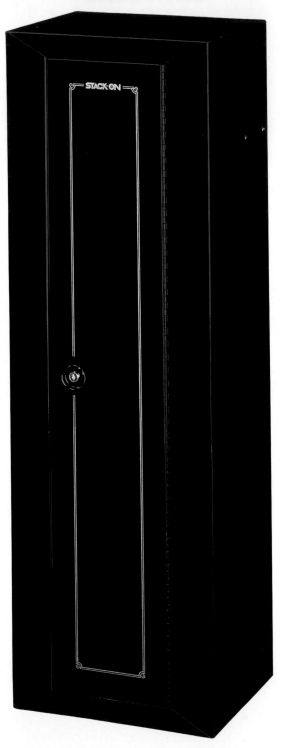

Stack-On 10 gun compact steel security cabinet

Gun security should be a primary issue for all owners, as firearms are often targeted during home burglaries along with jewelry, electronics, cash, and other easily disposed-of goods. Most solutions are inexpensive and easy to apply.

Security in the Home and Office

Keeping firearms away from unauthorized users is essential to everyone's security agenda. Think family members, neighbors, deliverymen, or maintenance workers who have access to your home from time to time. Whether we're talking one gun or many, you have several security options in a variety of price ranges.

Under the bed, in the top drawer of the nightstand, or in the dresser under your socks may have been customary locations for previous generations, but they're the first place someone will look for your gun. Where you are going to keep it should be a primary concern before you even buy a gun, an issue to discuss with your significant other or children.

Cost alone should not determine the best option for gun storage. It is only one factor of many. Buying a $10,000 safe to secure a couple of $500 guns may not sound financially prudent, but neither would storing a valuable set of antique Colt Paterson revolvers in a lockbox from a mass merchant.

Everyone has a budget, but beginning with a list of questions before making a security plan is a good place to start. With the budget as the bottom line, here are a few questions and options to consider:

1. Type of Guns

What type of guns do you have? If you are exclusively a defensive pistol shooter, a safe made primarily for shotguns and rifles is an exaggerated purchase. If you are a trap, skeet, or sporting-clay shooter with several shotguns, you will almost certainly need a stand-up safe.

Realize that what you own and shoot today may not be what you want to own and shoot two to three years from now. A safe or vault should be a serious investment. For a few hundred dollars more—pennies a day for a lifetime of security—consider flexibility, greater capacity, and more safety options than you immediately need. Hunting and the shooting sports are like any other fascinating and passionate pastime. The more you become enmeshed in any community, the more you will begin to expand the quality and diversity of tools.

An inexpensive safe with an electronic lock and override key bolted to a book or closet shelf will provide security for a couple of pistols. This little vault may not prevent a determined thief from prying it open. A year from now, when you purchase a rifle or shotgun, that small safe may not be sufficient. You'll want another safe; one better able to meet your changing needs. That's when you'll realize that for a few dollars more you could have purchased a larger model with plenty of room for handguns, paperwork, jewelry, and long guns.

2. Size of Safe

What do you need to secure? Firearms, of course, but think of your other valuables: jewelry, coin collections, family heirlooms, and important paperwork (birth certificates, passports, stock certificates, bonds, military discharge, and deed to the house). With little in the way of valuables, a small-to-medium safe is practical. Living with a big family may require a more substantial investment. Having space to include valuables like those precious love letters your wife sent while you were overseas is worth more in the long run than a few hundred extra dollars.

Safes can be bulky and heavy. That makes the purchase a negotiable family decision, especially if you are going to take the additional precaution of bolting it to the floor or wall. If it is a floor-mounted model, someone has to vacuum around it or wipe off the dust. Having a safe brings up other issues as well such as which family members get the combination and keys.

3. Decorative or Protective

There is a difference between a hulking steel box and a beautiful mahogany gun case with a decorative, acid-etched glass door. Among other things, one is relatively secure while the other is easy to penetrate. A wooden case, no matter how exotic, would not withstand a fire. For firearms security, safety always trumps good looks.

At a hunting lodge, an open gun rack is perfect at the end of a day. Like any enthusiasts in any sport, hunters want to compare guns and scopes, brag about their successes, and blame failures on something else. While a glass-front display case may have been appropriate a half-century ago, that is no longer the case. Reconfigure such cases to hold collectibles, rare books, or the family china, but for firearms, think less attractive and more protected.

Aware of the ying-yang of appearance versus strength, safe manufacturers try to design a beaugtiful and elegant safe that can be an attractive feature in home décor and make a nice addition to a room. Nevertheless, a safe can be an imposing piece of furniture.

4. Weight

For your needs, you may find that the right safe is also a heavy safe. Before purchasing such a safe one should seek professional guidance about floor-support strength, even if your single-story home is built on a cement pad. Once a 2,000-pound vault is set in place and the movers depart, adjusting it to retrieve a whining kitten that managed to squeeze in behind it is no easy matter.

No one wants to have his 2,000-pound safe go crashing through the floor when a tremor shakes the foundation or a graduation party's dancing and music create a pocket of structural instability. Just make sure to check with a qualified structural engineer to find out what would be appropriate placement for your home.

5. Fire

According to the Federal Bureau of Investigation, more than two million homes are burglarized each year. A strong safe may prevent your firearms from being pilfered. In today's tenuous legal climate, a stolen firearm traced to a subsequent felony can become an expensive and emotional legal hassle. (Whether or not you believe the police might recover your stolen property, you must file a report. Your insurance company and personal lawyer will also demand it.)

In contrast to burglaries, the National Fire Protection Association says that half a million homes catch fire every year. Remember, it can take only a few minutes for the average house to become an inferno. You will not have time to open the safe to grab guns and valuables. Instead, get the family out of the house and call 911 from somewhere safe. Smoke can quickly make breathing impossible. An all too commonly unknown truth is that people do not only die from the flames of a fire; they die because they inhale super-heated smoky vapors filled with ash, plastic residue, and other chemicals.

Just as important as protecting your loved ones, protecting your valuables will not be accomplished with a poorly made safe. Imagine the time and expense of replacing birth certificates, passports, deeds, jewelry, and firearms. Imagine the endless irritation of dealing with numerous government agencies, not to mention insurance companies.

When it comes to protecting guns from fire, you should read and understand the labels because every safe is not created equally. On the other hand, every quality product is well marked with the level of protection afforded and the certifying agency. (A high-quality safe or residential security container [RSC] from a reputable company will make the investment in time and money, and perhaps reputation, to have its products tested by an independent certification agency such as Underwriters Laboratories. Just know that this rating effort is strictly voluntary.)

Several private testing companies offer product certification for fire protection and a safe or vault will be labelled, for instance "1200 degrees for 45 minutes." Underwriters Laboratories (UL) and Intertek (ETL) evaluate safes. UL, the most frequently seen certification label in the US, is a worldwide safety- consulting and certification company. UL provides safety-related validation, testing, and training services to a wide range of clients, from manufacturers to government regulators and private insurance companies. ETL on the other hand actually allows consumers to confirm a seller's claim for fire protection. You might think that one purchasing consideration is how much you trust your local firefighters to respond in a timely manner, but it is best to assume that you will need more rather than less protection.

Safes and vaults defend against fire with layers of fireboard and thick steel. "Fireboard" is drywall with a layer of fiberglass reinforcing the gypsum. More fireboard layers and thicker steel plus a good door seal give your firearms better protection and, of course, cost more.

6. Insurance

Prior to purchasing a safe, it is important to review your home and auto insurance policies and speak with your agent (and even your community association, if any, which may have an insurance option). A policy may stipulate a UL standard or certification. A home or office safe sold in the US may come with a UL rating, which, in case of a loss, will determine the amount or percentage of your recovery.

Here is the UL Burglary Classification listing for a combination-locked safe. Each level adds protection and value . . . at a price:

TL-15: 15 minutes of protection against common mechanical and electrical hand tools.
TL-30: upgrades to 30 minutes of protection.
TRTL-30: 30 minutes of protection, but adds cutting torches.
TRTL-60: upgrades to 60 minutes of protection.
TXTL-60: 60 minutes of protection, but adds high explosives.

Most commercially sold firearm safes and vaults are classified—as far as protection of contents are concerned—as "Residential Security Containers." When buying a safe, beware of a rating scale created solely by the manufacturer because it has no correlation to any industry-recognized standard. A safe advertised as "Theft Resistant" may simply come with a cheap, dangling combination lock. No other protection level is guaranteed or implied and it may be no more resistant to a thief than a locked file cabinet.

Most safes or vaults sold to gun owners are actually Residential Security Containers and you may note "RSC" with a TL-5 rating. Such a UL-rated container is certified to withstand only a beating by one man wielding a hammer or hatchet and small crowbar for up to five minutes. Safes of this type, regardless of their cost, tend to list their steel thickness by "gauge." Common gauges for safes promoted to gun owners range from 10 to 20, thin to thinner.

Liberty Deluxe 17

Tips on purchasing a safe are to "buy up," buy heavy, and ensure that quoted wall thicknesses are steel rather than a combination of steel and coated wall board.

7. Access

How much access do you need—and how quickly—to your firearms? If you are a weekend deer hunter, a heavy-duty safe in your locked garage may be sufficient. If your purpose is personal protection, a sturdy safe that offers rapid access to a handgun is worth considering. The time it takes for criminals to enter your home can be short; so be sure to consider your personal needs for access when deciding on a safe or storage device.

Several companies have developed options for securing firearms while still providing owners with quick access. Depending on their size, these smaller safes also provide hidden storage for additional valuables and keep prying hands at bay.

Exteriors are typically only 16-gauge steel, about .06 inches thick and inside they're lined with protective foam. That's sturdy enough to secure a gun from the casual thief looking to grab something and run.

Relatively affordable, protective small safes can be mounted under a table or on a bookshelf. Features and options include separate override key locks, a tamper indicator, interior light, spring-loaded door, 9-volt battery operation with low-battery warning, motion detector and audio alarm, and additional security cables.

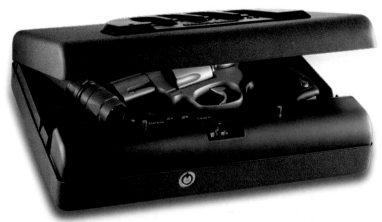

GunVault
MVB500-STD
MicroVault
Biometric
Pistol Safe

8. Wall Safes

Wall safes are popular in movies. Hidden behind painted mountain landscapes, they seem secure, invisible. If you are capable of doing a little woodworking (or don't mind calling a licensed and bonded carpenter) and have space in the right location, a wall safe may be right for you.

The value of a wall safe is that it remains hidden. While everyone walking into a room can spot a floor-mounted safe or gun cabinet, the location of a wall safe can be more difficult to detect. Wall safes are generally much smaller and therefore hold fewer valuables than the floor-mounted models. In addition, they are usually lightweight, with thin-gauge steel, which means that their fire-protection and burglary prevention is less.

WEST2114

Additional Safe-Buying Considerations

1. Although they are not the most important of all considerations, locks play an important role in gun security. Locks—and your ability to remember combinations or key in a security code or find a key under pressure—determine how quickly you can access your guns, if unwanted intruders are kept out, if it can be opened during a power outage, and, ultimately, the life of your safe and its contents.

There are two types of locks: electronic and mechanical. Electronic locks may require circuits, keypads, biometric scanners, and more while mechanical comes in the form of a key lock, a combination lock, or even dual locks. Electronic locks are powered by a battery, which must be regularly checked and replaced. These locks are quick and efficient but often last less than five years. Mechanical locks, on the other hand, tend to be bulky, tedious to handle, and open slowly. On the plus side they require little to no maintenance with little to no care while lasting a lifetime.

2. Many safes include interior outlets for 110 (240 in Europe), RJ45, and USB ports to plug in items such as dehumidifier rods and electronics without drilling after-market holes through the safe body. (Dehumidifier rods, recommended, generate a low level of heat that removes moisture from the air.)

3. Look for adjustable shelving, padded interior flooring, an accessory door-component hanger or shelving, and interior lighting for dim-light access.

4. Study the safe's warranty for duration, repair, parts replacement, and movement inside the home. Will a representative repair the safe in place or must it be returned to a dealer? Is the warranty transferrable if the safe is sold?

5. Individual needs may include jewelry trays, pistol racks and rifle rods, desiccants and/or dehumidifiers, black-powder warning stickers, motion sensors and tampering alarms, special "cool pockets" for accessory items, and lighting kits. If recommended by the manufacturer, make sure that it is bolted as securely to the floor and/or wall as possible.

The Soft-Sided Case

Soft-sided gun cases are popular with every shooter for their simplicity, easy storage, and excellent short-term firearm protection. Some soft cases come with accessory pockets for ammunition, cleaning kits, shotgun choke tubes, or anything else that you may need at the range or during a long day in the field. Some soft gun cases can serve as a range bag and gun case in one package while providing secure storage during transportation to and from a shooting area.

Though a soft case may be appropriate for temporary storage or a quick trip, it is not suitable for long-term gun storage. Although there are hundreds of sizes and styles for all types of handguns and long guns, a firearm left inside for too long will almost certainly begin to oxidize (rust) on worn surfaces. And because most cases are padded and felt-lined, any oils or solvents that drip from the gun will eventually damage the case.

Allen S&W M&P Tactical Rifle Case 42

SAFETY DEVICES FOR FIREARMS

Though firearm accident deaths among adults and children have decreased dramatically over a period of decades, and now are more uncommon than ever before, it is still important that gun owners give due consideration to their individual circumstances, and make solid decisions about the steps they can take to prevent unauthorized persons from obtaining their firearms. They should also know that there is no one method that will work equally well for every gun owner.

A good safety plan can begin with a firearm safety course (see NRA Training Chapter) to include, as needed, other members of the family.

Thereafter, a family that has small children or curious teenagers that have not yet been trained in the safe handling of firearms, or that lives in a neighborhood with a high burglary rate, may decide to keep their firearms locked in a safe or vault (see Firearms Storage chapter).

Not every safe weighs a thousand pounds or costs thousands of dollars. Small and inexpensive locking boxes, which can be bolted to the floor, can prevent anyone from easily gaining access to a firearm.

Though not as secure as a safe, there are other devices that provide a measure of security.

In 1988, the NRA launched the Eddie Eagle GunSafe Program. Created by past NRA President Marion P. Hammer in consultation with elementary school teachers, law enforcement officers, and child psychologists, Eddie Eagle teaches children, "If you see a gun: STOP! Don't Touch. Run Away. Tell a Grown-Up." Since 1988, more than twenty-eight million pre-K through fourth grade kids have received this lifesaving message.

Mechanical safety devices can never be absolutely relied upon to prevent an accidental discharge. After loading, abandoning a firearm for any reason—to get a cup of coffee, make a sandwich, or answer the telephone—is not acceptable.

Trigger locks are simple devices designed to keep guns from firing. While there are many styles, the most common type fits around and through a gun's trigger guard and uses interlocking rods to prevent the trigger from being pulled. Like a padlock, a trigger lock requires a key or a combination to be removed. It is not suitable for a loaded gun. Indeed, trigger locks are the focus of some criticism because a semi-automatic handgun or revolver can still be loaded and, if the lock is installed improperly, the gun could still fire. Nevertheless, when used properly, a trigger lock is an inexpensive safety investment. (Keep the key or combination to the safe in a separate location from that of the trigger lock.) Remington's key-operated Trigger Block is built with a hardened steel-center locking post and rubber insert pads to prevent scratching.

 Child Guard's key-locking CS-100 is a step forward in single-gun security, although not a "one-size-fits-all" solution to keeping kids safe from unauthorized use. The CS-100's movable safety posts allow you to fit the unit to a specific firearm, and moving the CS-100 from gun to gun takes only a minute or two. Its flexible design securely fits rifles, shotguns, pistols, and revolvers. There is nothing in front of the trigger that can fire the gun, nothing down the barrel that can scratch or damage it, and no floppy cable that might damage the finish. The CS-100 is lightweight and reinforced with tungsten carbide for exceptional cut resistance and strength without compromising the possible need for quick emergency use for self-defense.

An example of a trigger lock

Firearms can also be secured with a cable. These are generally fed through the magazine well and out the ejection port of a semi-auto handgun or rifle, preventing it from being loaded and fired. Swing the cylinder out and the cable works just as well for a revolver. The cable is then locked through the receiver. For the budget-minded gun owner a single cable can even be used for multiple guns. The wire cable of Remington's Cable Lock is protected by hardened steel beads that offer flexibility with some protection against cutting and sawing. The shrink-wrapped vinyl cable covering and full plastic lock body cover are designed to prevent them from scratching your firearms.

An example of a small, quick -access gun safe

Trigger locks and safety cables are designed to prevent accidental discharges. They will not prevent a determined adult who has access to cable cutters or a hammer or hacksaw from stealing and using your gun. And so they are useful elements only in the gun security puzzle, not total solutions.

Above and below are examples of how padlocks and cable locks can be used to prevent a firearm from functioning.

Chamber-View's bright orange plastic plug fits through the ejection port and into the chamber of most long guns. The plug provides immediate visual recognition that a firearm has been rendered safe. Originally introduced for shotguns, the popular plug has also been developed in sizes and shapes for rifles and handguns.

149

CAUTION: Federal and state firearms laws are subject to frequent change. This summary is not to be considered as legal advice or a restatement of law. To determine the applicability of these laws to specific situations that you may encounter, you are strongly urged to consult a local attorney.

Not long ago it was common to see hunters driving along the countryside with a rifle or shotgun at their side (or in their gun rack). It was a popular practice in rural areas where traffic was light, hunters knew their neighbors, and game wardens were lenient. Times have changed.

About Traveling

Traveling locally, you must abide by local, state, and federal law. Depending on state law and whether or not you have a carry permit, you may be able to carry a loaded firearm in the passenger compartment of your vehicle. Local law may also add additional restrictions, however, many states have firearm "preemption" laws that prohibit localities from further regulating the possession of firearms. It's important to be aware of the many variations in state law because several states require firearms to be transported in a completely secure manner. For example, a few states require any firearm being transported to be unloaded and either locked in a secure container or locked in a separate compartment of the transporting vehicle, and, even then, the firearm can only be transported for limited purposes such as going to or from a shooting range or gunsmith's shop.

Except in rural areas, the days of gun racks in the back windows of pickups are essentially over. Because states have varying laws about concealed carry, you should not have your legally owned handgun in the passenger compartment when you cross state lines unless you are certain to be in compliance with the laws of your destination state and any state you pass through. While there is a federal law that generally provides for the safe interstate transportation of firearms notwithstanding state law, if the firearm is otherwise lawfully possessed and stored in compliance with federal law, several states have embarrassingly poor records of complying with this law, so for your own legal protection, you must know their laws and abide by them.

Most trips will be within the neighborhood, in the car or truck to a hunt club or a skeet range, but there will be times when you want to travel across state lines for hunting, a competition, or perhaps you are moving for a new job. In each case, prior thought can prevent time-consuming and expensive legal hassles later.

In a camper, van, or motor home, where driving and living spaces are restricted, the same issue of "accessibility" is more complex. In such a case the federal interstate transportation law and the laws of some states require that any firearms are unloaded and the firearms and ammunition are secured in a locked container.

No Federal Permit Required, But . . .

As a responsible gun owner, you are required to know and comply with all local, state, and federal laws. There is no uniform state firearms transportation protocol, but some localities have passed laws restricting transportation. Possession of a valid concealed-carry permit from one state does not mean that it is acceptable across the border.

Federal law does not restrict an individual from transporting firearms across state lines and does not require a permit. The only people who are specifically restricted are generally: individuals with certain criminal convictions, the mentally ill, drug users, illegal aliens, veterans dishonorably discharged, those who have renounced their US citizenship, respondents to certain protective orders, and fugitives from justice.

Here are a few examples cited in NRA publications that illustrate the varying nature of state and local laws, examples that should cause gun owners to inquire, in advance, about travel requirements:

CALIFORNIA—California has extensive state and local regulatory schemes over firearms and ammunition. For more specific information, please contact the Department of Justice Firearms Bureau at (916) 263-4887, or at www.ag.ca.gov/firearms

HAWAII—Every person arriving into the state who brings a firearm of any description, usable or not, shall register the firearm within three days of the arrival of the person or the firearm, whichever arrives later, with the chief of police of the county where the person will reside, where their business is, or the person's place of sojourn. For more information, visit www.hawaiipolice.com/services/firearm-registration

MASSACHUSETTS—Massachusetts imposes harsh penalties on the mere possession and transport of firearms unrelated to criminal or violent conduct. Prospective travelers are urged to contact the Massachusetts Firearms Records Bureau at (617) 660-4780 or the State Police at www.mass.gov/msp/firearms/ for further information.

NEW JERSEY—New Jersey has highly restrictive firearms laws. The New Jersey Supreme Court has ruled that anyone traveling within the state is deemed to be aware of these regulations and will be held strictly accountable for violations. From New Jersey State Police regarding transporting firearms through the state: www.state.nj.us/njsp/about/fire_trans.html

NEW YORK—Use extreme caution when traveling through New York with firearms. New York State's general approach is to make the possession of handguns and so-called "assault weapons" and "large capacity ammunition feeding devices" illegal and then provide exceptions that the accused may raise as "affirmative defenses" to prosecution in some cases.

A number of localities, including Albany, Buffalo, New York City, Rochester, Suffolk County, and Yonkers, impose their own requirements on the possession, registration, and transport of firearms. Possession of a handgun within New York City requires a New York City handgun license or a special permit from the city police commissioner validating a state license within the city. Even New York state licenses are generally not valid within New York City unless a specific exemption applies, such as when the New York City police commissioner has issued a special permit to the licensee or "the firearms covered by such license are being transported by the licensee in a locked container and the trip through the city of New York is continuous and uninterrupted." Possession of a shotgun or rifle within New York City requires a permit, which is available to non-residents, and a certificate of registration.

Flying with Firearms

Though you can't fly with a firearm on your person, you can transport firearms on a plane. Legally. You need a tough, hard-sided case for your rifle or shotgun and perhaps extra patience when traveling to Africa for a safari or Spain for sporting-clays shoot. Most international travel forbids carrying a handgun. And no matter what—every gun must be declared, unloaded, locked in a hard-sided case and checked through with baggage. Traveling with firearms prohibits you from those convenient curbside check-ins. Airguns, paintball equipment, and other such gear are not technically firearms, but the quicker you declare them and clarify any issues with your airline the better.

Ammunition can be shipped as long as it is packed separately from your gun in your checked luggage. Airlines often have limits on the amount (by weight and caliber, .75 being the maximum) that can be transported. This especially affects shotgun events in which participants will shoot several boxes a day at international competitions or a South American dove field. Here, as an example of the regulations for travel with firearms and ammunition, is the TSA summary for transporting guns:

To avoid issues that could impact your travel and/or result in law enforcement action, here are some guidelines to assist you in packing your firearms and ammunition:
• All firearms must be declared to the airline during the ticket counter check-in process.
• The term firearm includes: *Please see, for instance, United States Code, Title 18, Part 1, Chapter 44 for information about firearm definitions.
• Any weapon (including a starter gun) which will, or is designed to, or may readily be converted to expel a projectile by the action of an explosive.
• The frame or receiver of any such weapon.
• Any firearm muffler or firearm silencer.
• Any destructive device.
• The firearm must be unloaded.
• As defined by 49 CFR 1540.5 - "A loaded firearm means a firearm that has a

live round of ammunition, or any component thereof, in the chamber or cylinder or in a magazine inserted in the firearm."

- The firearm must be in a hard-sided container that is locked. A locked container is defined as one that completely secures the firearm from being accessed. Locked cases that can be pulled open with little effort cannot be brought aboard the aircraft.
- If firearms are not properly declared or packaged, TSA will provide the checked bag to law enforcement for resolution with the airline. If the issue is resolved, law enforcement will release the bag to TSA so screening may be completed.
- TSA must resolve all alarms in checked baggage. If a locked container containing a firearm alarms, TSA will contact the airline, who will make a reasonable attempt to contact the owner and advise the passenger to go to the screening location. If contact is not made, the container will not be placed on the aircraft.
- If a locked container alarms during screening and is not marked as containing a declared firearm, TSA will cut the lock in order to resolve the alarm.
- Travelers should remain in the area designated by the aircraft operator or TSA representative to take the key back after the container is cleared for transportation.
- Travelers must securely pack any ammunition in fiber (such as cardboard), wood or metal boxes or other packaging specifically designed to carry small amounts of ammunition.
- Firearm magazines and ammunition clips, whether loaded or empty, must be securely boxed or included within a hard-sided case containing an unloaded firearm.
- Small arms ammunition, including ammunition not exceeding .75 caliber for a rifle or pistol and shotgun shells of any gauge, may be carried in the same hard-sided case as the firearm, as long as it follows the packing guidelines described above.
- TSA prohibits black powder or percussion caps used with black powder.
- Rifle scopes are not prohibited in carry-on bags and do not need to be in the hard-sided, locked checked bag.

Guns & Firearms

Item	Carry-on	Checked
Small arms ammunition, including ammunition up to .75 caliber and shotgun shells of any gauge - Check with your airline or travel agent to see if ammunition is permitted in checked baggage on the airline you are flying. Small arms ammunitions for personal use must be securely packaged in fiber, wood, or metal boxes or other packaging specifically designed to carry small amounts of ammunition. Ask about limitations or fees, if any, that apply.	No	Yes
BB guns	No	Yes
Compressed Air Guns, including rifles and pistols (to include paintball markers) - Carried in checked luggage without compressed air cylinder attached.	No	Yes
Firearms - Firearms carried as checked baggage MUST be unloaded, packed in a locked hard-sided container, and declared to the airline at check-in.	No	Yes
Flare Guns - May be carried as checked baggage and MUST be unloaded, packed in a locked hard-sided container, and declared to the airline at check-in. Read our section on Camping.	No	Yes
Flares	No	No
Gun Lighters	No	Yes
Gun Powder including black powder and percussion caps	No	No
Parts of Guns and Firearms (e.g., frames, receivers, ammunition clips, magazines)	No	Yes
Pellet Guns	No	Yes
Realistic Replicas of Firearms	No	Yes
Starter Pistols - Can only be carried as checked baggage and MUST be unloaded, packed in a locked hard-sided container, and declared to the airline at check-in.	No	Yes

NOTE: Check with your airline or travel agent to see if firearms are permitted in checked baggage on the airline you are flying. Ask about limitations or fees, if any, that apply.

Right: Pelican's black 1770 transport case

The Case for Travel

A hard case with heavy foam cushioning is the best option for securing guns when it comes to international travel. You will probably have to cut the foam to the precise dimensions of your gun. These cases usually have separate compartments for magazines and accessories, but the ammo must be stored separately.

While Transportation Security Agents may visually inspect the interior of your firearms case, they are not allowed to handle your gun. If they ask for permission to handle your gun you can either politely refuse or allow them a quick look. If they believe anything is amiss, they can summon a credentialed law enforcement officer for additional inspection. You may be asked why you are traveling with a firearm and a simple, polite answer—"I'm hunting buffalo in Tanzania" or "I'm attending a trap and skeet shoot in Venezuela"—is usually the end of the inspection.

Your gun will then become general checked luggage (sometimes they are routed to special handling at your destination). Fly direct if possible to avoid secondary handling or mishandling. Once you arrive, find a gate agent and ask where to pick up "special luggage." (In today's political climate, patience and humor will be your greatest security—and that of your firearms as well—in any international travel.) Experienced travelers complete a US Customs form 4457, Certificate of Registration for Personal Effects Taken Abroad, in advance of arriving at the airport, especially for a foreign-produced item. Here are two cases that fit the needs of travel with firearms:

• Pelican's black 1770 Transport Case is practically unbreakable, watertight, airtight, dustproof, chemical resistant, and corrosion-proof. Made of "Ultra High Impact structural copolymer" for strength and durability, it seals with a ¼-inch neoprene O-ring, has an automatic purge valve for quick equalization after changes in atmospheric pressure, and uses double-throw lockable latches. It comes with two handles and built-in polyurethane wheels with stainless steel bearings.

• Boyt's high-impact, injection-molded Tactical H-Series Single-Rifle Case is designed for travel with a high-performance rifle. It weighs 18.5 pounds and uses customizable, high-density foam to protect your gun. It, too, has a pressure-relief valve, a waterproof and dustproof O-ring.

NRA Training Opportunities

Many courses in safe and effective handling of firearms are available all around the country, but those offered by the National Rifle Association (NRA) are among the very best. Whether you are a new gun owner, a hunter looking to expand your expertise, or a citizen determined to protect your home, the NRA's Education and & Training Division has the course for you.

The NRA Education & Training Division develops safe, ethical, responsible shooters through a network of more than one hundred thousand instructors, range-safety officers, coaches, and training counselors. NRA Training Counselors recruit and train instructors who teach NRA's basic firearm courses. NRA Coaches, in turn, develop competitors at the club, high school, collegiate, and national levels.

For those interested in joining the millions of NRA members who hunt, the NRA offers a wide range of programs addressing all aspects of hunting including the Youth Hunter Education Challenge, advanced skills training, and the conservation of our natural and wildlife resources. All Hunter Services Department programs work toward the common goal of instilling and promoting the skills and ethics that will ensure the continuance of America's proud hunting heritage.

It hasn't always been easy for women to break into the shooting sports. But now programs like NRA's Women On Target Instructional Shooting Clinic make the break an easy one (www.women.nra.org and www.nrawomen.tv). Whether interested in personal safety, gun safety, gun knowledge, marksmanship, hunting, or recreational or competitive shooting, the NRA has a variety of programs and activities that encourage female participation at all skill levels.

The NRA also helps adult leaders and national youth programs—such as the Boy Scouts of America and 4-H—develop shooting curriculums. NRA programs provide all shooters with a lifetime of recreational and competitive opportunities, as well as developing programs for NRA youth members and NRA-affiliated youth clubs.

Two NRA Programs Merit Special Attention:

• The NRA America's Rifle Challenge is a training event designed to develop modern, practical rifle skills with general-purpose rifles, such as the AR-15. Challenge events are designed for shooters of all skill levels and can be conducted on almost any centerfire range. Attendees learn safe firearm-handling skills with their personal firearms and gear; then they demonstrate their athletic and tactical abilities in real-world skill sets.

• NRA short-term gunsmithing schools offer courses on topics such as general gunsmithing, bluing, stockmaking, checkering, engraving, and parkerizing. More specialized courses focus on topics such as accurizing the AR-15 rifle; accurizing varmint rifles; fine-tuning single-action revolvers and long guns for cowboy shoots; accurizing the Colt Model 1911 pistol; and English gunsmithing. Law enforcement armorer classes are also offered.

To join the National Rifle Association or for additional information regarding membership or the always-adapting course structure, call (800) NRA-3888 or visit http://membership.nrahq.org/. Membership dues can be charged to VISA, MasterCard, American Express, or Discover.

NATIONAL RIFLE ASSOCIATION

Short-Term Gunsmithing Schools

Current NRA Courses

The NRA develops courses based on need and adaptation to fluid national situations. A Basic Defensive Pistol course, for example, has been developed thanks to increased interest and a determination that the public will benefit from this particular brand of expert instruction.

Basic Safety and Gun Handling

NRA has courses available to fit most needs, from the first time-buyer to the experienced shooter who is simply looking to increase their knowledge, or satisfy any myriad of training requirements. For recreational shooters, competition, hunting, gun collecting, personal protection—the basics are the place to start. NRA Basic Firearm Training courses teach the principles of safe handling and marksmanship, and instill the appropriate knowledge, skills, and attitude that will last a lifetime. Some courses can be taken in the comfort of your own home, in an eLearning environment, while others may be presented in a blended format—which means a large portion is completed at your own pace, at home using your computer, followed by a practical requirement completed in person with a certified instructor to earn your completion certificate.

There are courses available in every shooting discipline, as well as non-shooting courses like Range Safety Officer, Reloading, Home Firearm Safety, and Refuse To Be A Victim®. NRA courses can last anywhere from three hours to a couple days, depending on the discipline you choose. For example, NRA has a three-hour orientation for one specific firearm that is referred to as FIRST Steps. FIRST is an acronym for Firearm, Instruction, Responsibility and Safety Training. This course was developed to train individuals that purchased their first gun, without any prior knowledge or training. By the time they earn their certificate, they should be able to safely handle (load, unload, cock, and decock) their personal firearm, shoot it well and learn to clean it. On the other hand, NRA also offers courses through advanced Personal Protection Outside The Home for experienced shooters which teaches the appropriate knowledge, skills, and attitude essential for avoiding dangerous confrontations and for the safe, effective, responsible, and ethical use of a concealed pistol for self-defense.

NRA even works in conjunction with the National Muzzle Loading Rifle Association (NMLRA) to provide training for primitive type guns—loaded from the muzzle, using black powder or appropriate substitute. Muzzleloading guns played a major role in shaping American history, and the tradition of shooting them in competition, hunting and recreation lives on through the joint efforts of the NRA and NMLRA. Additional information on muzzleloading can be obtained directly from the NMLRA at nmlra.org.

Experienced shooters that are looking for ways to increase the number of bullets they send downrange each year on the same shooting budget they are accustomed to, may want to consider reloading their own ammunition. If that's the case, NRA offers one-day courses on metallic and shotgun shell reloading.

One of NRA's most interesting courses does not even include firearms. The Refuse To Be A Victim® course teaches you to be a hard target–developing a personal safety strategy to avoid situations that could change your life in an instant, whether it is through identity theft, scams, or situations that would require a level of self-defense. The neat thing about the Refuse To Be A Victim® course is that it is tailored to an individual or groups specific needs, such as college students, senior citizens, school teachers, women-only, and so on. There is even a special module for parents that discuss tips for children ages pre-school to college.

The bottom line, if you are interested in learning about shooting, personal protection, hunting, recreation, collecting, competition . . . the list goes on, it's likely that NRA has a program and material appropriate for you. NRA has made it easy to find a course as well. All you need to do is visit nrainstructors.org.

Once you are at nrainstructors.org, check the boxes for the courses you are interested in and search for them using your zip code. After finding a course, registering for it is simple. When you arrive to attend the course, instructors will provide you with appropriate training material, which is described in the course catalog at nrainstructors.org. Once you pass the course, you should be provided with a course completion certificate bearing the signature of the NRA Secretary.

INDEX